A NEW WAY TO ~~LIKE~~ LOVE YOUR NEIGHBOR

A NEW WAY ~~LIKE~~ LOVE TO YOUR NEIGHBOR

Be Curious, Free, and Brave—
How to Transform Your
Relationship with God and Others

JADA EDWARDS

B&H
PUBLISHING®
BRENTWOOD, TENNESSEE

978-1-0877-8918-7

Published by B&H Publishing Group
Brentwood, Tennessee

Published in association with Yates & Yates, LLP. www.yates2.com

Dewey Decimal Classification: 302
Subject Heading: NEIGHBORS / INTERPERSONAL RELATIONS /
GOD (CHRISTIANITY)—LOVE

Cover design by B&H Publishing Group.
Author photo by Desmond Hunt (Dlores Media Group).

1 2 3 4 5 • 28 27 26 25

To Conway: You are my favorite neighbor.
It is a privilege to love you.

To Joah and Chloe: In His grace, God has
allowed me to be your mother.
You have taught me that love is the most
important anchor in a relationship.
You have forever changed me, and I hope
you never doubt my love for you.

To One Community Church: You are an ever-evolving joy.
I am deeply grateful for our journey. You are home.

Contents

Introduction

If you've picked up this book, you're probably interested in either being loved well or loving others well—or both. More than that, you're probably curious about how this "new way" to love might affect your life.

What is this new way? What does it entail? Is it realistic? Will it be worth the effort? Does it even matter to you? I'm guessing it does. Most of us believe that being a "loving" person is directly connected to be a "good" person. When people speak about us, we all want to hear that we were kind, compassionate, reliable, safe, and so many other adjectives to sum up love. You don't have to be a high-touch, deeply emotive, constantly smiling kind of person to want that said about you. There aren't many people (if any) that want to be remembered for their moodiness, self-centeredness, grudge-holding, or emotional disconnection. The real question isn't *if* you and I want to be loved or love others well. The question is *how*.

I've been on a long personal journey exploring that question, and it all started with the story I'm going to tell a few paragraphs from now. But before we jump into it, let's cover two things.

The first thing you need to know is I'm coming at this subject from a Christian perspective. I believe God is the source of love and can teach us all we need to know about it. He is the epitome of love, so to not consider Him or His Word seems unwise for such an important topic. I know many religions and cultures have varying ideas of love, but truthfully, it all starts and ends with God. Human love is informed by, and can only flow from, divine love, so considering the "divine" part of the equation matters a great deal. And in so many ways, it's exactly what makes strong and enduring human love possible. I mean, even if you aren't a spiritual person, you can at least admit that the way our world loves doesn't work out over the long term. It may make sense for a generation or two, but eventually we change and so do our values, wants, and needs. Divine love is the necessary anchor. It doesn't negate human love, but it grounds it. What if considering the spiritual angle helps us approach it in a whole new way? If this isn't your comfort zone or your norm, I challenge you to give it some meaningful consideration. You might be pleasantly surprised and hopefully forever changed.

The second thing to know is this book is not geared primarily toward romantic love or love experienced within a marriage. It can certainly apply in those realms, but I worked hard to present this work in a way that helps us be better at love in *every* kind of relationship. Relationships with our family, friends, coworkers, roommates, classmates, neighbors, church family, hairstylists, bank tellers, committee leaders, dog groomers, social media commenters, and so on. Why? Because, as I said before, it doesn't take long to look around at our society and see that we've got a love issue in almost *every* relationship. With a simple comment on a social media post, you notice someone assassinating another person's character or questioning their humanity. You witness a neighbor ready to go to battle over a poorly parked car or a joke that didn't include them. You realize your roommate is passive-aggressively leaving dishes in the sink or not honoring your space. You notice your classmate stealing your work and calling it their own.

Or maybe *you're* the one creating the difficulties and you can't seem to pinpoint why. You're sad about the fact that you keep lashing out at that same person (or unsuspecting strangers) time after time, even though you weren't planning to. You're frustrated that you can't seem to keep your mouth shut when the time comes to avoid gossip. You're wondering why you keep having the same petty fight with your spouse or your friend. You're still harboring jealousy or annoyance for that one coworker. You can't seem to heal from that betrayal.

Third thing, this is not meant to be a step-by-step guide to your relationship. It's meant to establish a foundation or philosophy which becomes the starting point. If a relationship is already toxic or feels beyond hope or even unsafe—don't think new behavior will change things overnight. I am focused on new hearts and new thinking in this book. From there, I have no doubt God will guide your next step. But go to Him first. Think like Him. Chase His perspective.

Here's the thing, all these people are your neighbors in life—not just the people who live next to you. Yep, that's a lot of neighbors and a lot of love we need to be offering up, and it can be exhausting without a healthy perspective.

We've all been there and we're all growing, so I'm glad you picked up this book (or received it as a gift, or had it shoved in your hand). I want to invite you to learn with me. Join me on this journey but make it your own. I've been changed by some of the lessons I've learned along the way, and I'd love to share them with you. Don't get me wrong: I'm no superhuman. I'm so far from perfect, but I have found a new path, and that's all we can do. In the pages that follow, I will include a variety of stories, which pull from different kinds of relationships and others of which will be marriage related (like the one below). I love real-life stories because love is something we need to be expressing with every person we know, in all kinds of environments. If I do mention a marriage-related story, it isn't because this is a book focused on marriage. It's because my husband happens to be my closest "neighbor," and he is (unknowingly) teaching me how to embrace this new way to love.

All that being said, let's talk about how this whole thing started.

■ ■ ■

I was enjoying my time with God, telling Him everything that was on my heart, trying to listen to His guidance and His voice, and then it hit me. I had a thorough list of requests that

I needed God to handle soon. I was frustrated and growing resentful at how long it was taking. This particular evening, I was reminding Him of some work that still needed to be done . . . in my husband. It was in the middle of one of my most compelling arguments that I felt the Lord convicting me, essentially saying, *"Jada, you have a love problem."*

I agreed. "I know," I said. I knew I wasn't the softest, most compassionate person. This has always been a part of my life's work: cultivating deeper sympathy, attempting authentic presence with people, and bearing other's burdens at the direction of the Lord. So God got no argument from me. I heard the words, paused briefly to acknowledge them, and moved on with my "case" for that day. I was interrupted again with the same conviction from God. *"No. You don't understand. I'm not saying you have an issue with being loving. Jada, I'm saying the issue you keep bringing before me is itself a love issue."* This was the start to a gentle jolting. (That's what God does, you know.) God showed me that my "love issue" wasn't a matter of being more loving—as it relates to behavior or expression. It was about *what* I loved most and *how* I loved, which was absolutely a matter of the heart.

As the Spirit of God started to show me my motives, I realized that in that season, I loved my idea of marriage more than God. I loved what I wanted God to do in my husband— some future version of him—more than God Himself. And I loved my self-righteousness more than God.

Now, is it wrong to pray for God to do a work in a friend or a coworker or a spouse? Is it wrong to ask God to change someone's heart? No and no. Many times those kinds of prayers are God-led. So how did I know that my prayer in this particular season *wasn't* so godly? Because my heart was growing resentful the longer it took for God to respond in the way I wanted, and **resentment is never the fruit of pure-hearted prayer.** This was a reawakening for me. This disproportionate love started to show up in several areas of my life. I started noticing it not only in my relationship with my husband but in many of my other relationships. A few weeks later the Lord brought all this revelation full circle. He took me back to the familiar but foundational passage of Mark 12:28–31 (ESV):

> And one of the scribes came up and . . . asked him, "Which commandment is the most important of all?" Jesus answered, "The most important is, 'Hear, O Israel: The Lord our God, the Lord is one. And you shall love the Lord your God with all your heart and with all your soul and with all your mind and with all your strength.' The second is this: 'You shall love your neighbor as yourself.' There is no other commandment greater than these."

This left me with the overarching question, "I get this, and I want to do it. I want to love this way—the Jesus way. I want to love God and others in ways that require faith and selflessness. But I feel constrained all the time, like something is holding me back. So, how do I recognize and remove the limits that are holding me back? How can I love with my heart, soul, mind, and strength?"

My profound realization sent me on a journey to rediscover the idea of love that God demonstrates perfectly and commands us to model in our imperfection. There is much work to be done in understanding this, but the journey will be one that changes the way we see everything and everyone. I mean that. God shows us what love is supposed to look like, and when we catch His vision, it really does transform all our relationships. My journey may have started in my relationship with my husband, but loving according to God's design changes *any* kind of relationship, *all* our relationships, no exceptions. It changes the way you introduce yourself to strangers. It changes the way you engage with coworkers. It even changes the way you love your family and the friends you may have known for years. Whether the relationship is new or old, occasional or daily, professional or personal, it will be affected. It can change for the better. I'm talking about *every single relationship* in your life. **God's transformative way of doing love is not something to fear but something that somehow fills you even as you give freely.** Do you want that?

Me too. So let's start by exploring what's ahead of us in this book.

In part 1, we'll explore various limits that might be restricting your experience of receiving God's love (and giving it). We'll consider four limits that could be holding you back, and trust me: when you work to remove them, you'll not only enjoy God's deep and abiding love for you, but you'll also be able to be a vessel for that love for others in ways you never have before.

In part 2, we'll explore the natural result of experiencing God's unlimited love, which is what love looks like when it flows through you and into the lives of others. Put differently, you'll learn how to love others around you in a whole new way, a way the world doesn't expect and can't explain. A way that only God could empower. To be more specific, in a world that's disinterested, you'll be curious. In a world that locks itself in its own prison of unforgiveness and bitterness toward others, you'll be free and forgiving. In a world that is afraid and unable to feel discomfort, you'll have what it takes to be brave and uncomfortable. In a world that gives up at the first sight of difficulty in friendships, relational disputes, marriage challenges, and workplace disagreements, you'll be resilient. And in a world that is dishonest, power hungry, and often fake in its posture toward others, you'll be honest, humble, and real.

So let's learn some new things about love together—and watch our relationships transform as a result.

PART 1

What Is Limiting Your Love?

Chapter 1

LIMIT 1: Settling for the Wrong Definitions

Have you ever had someone ask you a broad, life-defining question like, "What's your favorite food?" or "What's your favorite color?" Maybe you've been asked to share your favorite movie or concert. I am often surprised at how some people are able to give immediate answers to these questions. When I am asked those questions, my mind starts to race through all of the variables that might determine my "favorite" thing, and inevitably I end up asking more questions. This may seem unnecessary but, hey, I need clarity. When it comes to a favorite food, I may ask if they are referring to breakfast, casual dinner, or sporting-event-concession-stand food. In my book, those are important qualifiers that provide different answers. When deciding a favorite color, I want to know which season or maybe which article of clothing. My favorite color for shirts is different from my favorite color for pants or dresses. Don't even get me started on concerts and movies. Do you want to know my favorite comedy movie or my favorite action movie or maybe my favorite documentary? Do you want to know my favorite singer or favorite band or favorite overall concert experience? These kinds of questions can lead to more questions because they are so broad. There are so many ways to define a "favorite," and there are so many variables that might change what your favorite thing is depending on the environment or the season or your mood. To be answered accurately, these questions need context and detail so a person can understand how to give the most precise answer to the question.

Something similar is happening when we talk about navigating the broad idea of love. We all want to navigate it well. We all want to show up to it with good habits, enjoy love, and give love in ways that are best for ourselves and others. But there's a way love is designed to be "lived," and if we paint with too broad of a stroke or fail to understand God's context, **we'll create our own definition and miss God's intention.** In addition to that, we'll be limited in how much we can enjoy it. We all have ideas about love, but our ability to enjoy it hinges on whether or not we're working with the right understanding of it.

In this chapter, we're going to explore the wrong *and* the right definition of love, and the way we'll do that is to look at three overarching problems that create gaps between the way we approach love and the way God designed us to.

Problem 1—We Have Too Many Ideas about Love

To begin with, we have so many different ideas about love and so many emotions that we call love, it's almost impossible to define. To explain my point, consider words like Kleenex, Band-Aid, ChapStick, or aspirin. These are words that were once trademarked to represent specific items. But as competition entered the market, these words became synonymous with an entire genre of products. No one asks for a facial tissue; they ask for Kleenex. People don't generally ask for an adhesive bandage or lip balm. They ask for a Band-Aid or ChapStick (maybe Carmex). And who ever asks for nonsteroidal anti-inflammatory drugs? Not me. I just ask for Aleve, Advil, or Motrin. My point is that instead of meaning something specific, these words now cover a wide range of items—and none of us think twice about it.

In English, a similar thing has happened with the word *love*. It *should* mean something specific, but instead it is now used to describe a wide spectrum of sentiments that get lumped together with one word. It covers personal affection, familial love, romantic feelings, worship and devotion, compassion and concern, sexual attraction, personal appreciation, personal preference, and more. We use the word so broadly, and sometimes so loosely, that it loses its meaning. We say we love our children and our spouses. We also love our pets, our cars, our hairstyles, and favorite foods. As a matter of fact, the *way* we say it can add to the nuance. A serious "I love you" outweighs a "Love ya" any day.

Technology has added to this broadness, as it gives us further avenues to express ourselves in bite-sized ways. You can "love" a message or image sent to your device. You can "heart" a comment or post on social media platforms. But that same heart icon can mean anything from a mild approval to passionate agreement. The way we so frequently, and sometimes frivolously, express affection can oversimplify the definition of love according to God. God's love is not a watered-down, diluted expression of affection. It is a high calling and a standard measured by sacrifice and consistency, which we will further unpack later in this book.

We've talked about some general ways we have too many ideas about love, but what are some specific ways this plays out? Let's explore three briefly below:

Love = Affection Based on Someone's Performance

When we speak about love in our relationships, we are typically speaking about some level of affection or affinity that can vary depending on the behavior of the object of our affection. For example, many of us feel like we love our spouses, kids, or friends more on the days they show us intentional care, while we feel less love for them on the days they seem distant. Whether we're referring to objects, people, or events, it is always a love that requires us to be satisfied with the performance of the other party before the affection can be present.

Love = A Grandiose, Romantic Idea that Can Save Us

Sometimes we think and speak of love as a general, intangible idea instead of a call to action as God intends. Events like weddings can send us into a fantastical, idealistic world where love is some indescribable, overwhelming reality that fills us to the point where it sustains us. It's a euphoric state of being. We can unknowingly idolize love as we talk about its power, its ability to heal, stabilize, and satisfy apart from the One who established love. Boiled down, we think the idea of love can save us when it simply can not.

Love = A Transaction Based on What Someone Offers

On the other hand, as opposed to generous or all-encompassing, we may merely imagine love as a transaction that is mutually beneficial in some way. We start out loving our parents because they provide for our basic needs. We build our early friendships because that friend makes us feel brave or has a talent we desire or understands our family. These relationships are based on what the other person offers to us. But as we mature, those relationships should evolve. If relationships don't move past a transactional identity, they typically *dissolve* rather than *evolve*. Eventually, we should love our parents because they are the gift God has given us, and He has asked us to honor them in all

> If relationships don't move past a transactional identity, they typically *dissolve* rather than *evolve*.

their imperfections. Likewise, we should have friendships based on mutual contribution with the understanding that when one friend fails, disappoints, or ceases to offer what we want, we seek God in His wisdom rather than disconnect from the friendship.

Love is more than receiving a benefit or feeling good. Often, we think it's the result of someone or something making us happy no matter how temporary or shallow. Other times we think it's simply a transaction, or a lofty idea floating around in the air that can save us, if we could just grab ahold of it. Those are the types of "love" we are drawn to; they feel natural to us.

We are not naturally drawn to the type of love that is not reciprocated or appreciated because we are not inclined to love sacrificially. (Fear not, *sacrificial* is not a code word for abusive or toxic.) If you are a parent, uncle, aunt, guardian, or the like, you undoubtedly have experienced a taste of sacrificial love toward the children in your life. But even as we try to love our children in sacrificial ways, we usually (if we're honest) expect a connection that benefits us in some way. The benefit may be a sense of identity, affirmation, affection, or something unnamed, but it's common for parents to need something from their kids. Don't get me wrong: it's normal and good to build bonds with your children. My point is that in every relationship human love generally wants some sort of "return on its investment."

So, when it comes to this first problem—too many ideas about love—what's the solution?

Solution 1: Choosing God's Definition of Love

If the world offers so many ideas about love, how can we find the right one? If we've been defining love in all the wrong ways and this has, in turn, limited our experience of love, then what's the right definition? God tells us clearly in His Word: "This is how God showed his love among us: He sent his one and only Son into the world that we might live through him" (1 John 4:9 NIV). This is the essence of the gospel. God who has loved us since creation desires relationship with us. When our sin severed the connection we had with God, He sent a solution to restore the broken relationship between Himself and humankind. The solution was the life, work, death, and resurrection of Jesus Christ. It wasn't easy and it wasn't cheap. And the mind-blowing truth is God did all of this out of His love for us. Not His *need* for us. Not His expectation of us. Not even His *use* for us. But simply, His *love* for us. That reality must be the backdrop to every pursuit of loving others, or we will always miss the mark.

Problem 2—We Define God's Love Based on Human Experiences

The second problem that creates gaps, or limits, between the way we love and the way God designed us to love is this: we are inclined to define love (God's love in particular) based on our human experiences. These experiences are largely set by our early childhood years. When our experiences of love are negative, this births pessimism or hopelessness and lowers our expectation for what God's love can do in our lives. Negative, traumatic experiences are almost always at the root of any unhealthy life patterns we find ourselves in as adults.

On the flip side, when our experiences are positive, we are filled with an idea of love that is sometimes overrated and romanticized in our own heads. For example, think about your own father. Whoever God sovereignly allowed to be your father has had lasting impact on you. You may have had a biological father who was amazing and loved the Lord, but I guarantee you he still fell short. Somewhere in your mind, however, he probably created the standard of what fatherly love is. On the other hand, you may have had a strained relationship with or have been abandoned by your earthly father, and that too will set a certain standard in your mind. That sort of pain will definitely leave a wound so deep it will taint the way you view love. Maybe your parents were married, but your father wasn't *present*. Then you would draw conclusions that could lead you to an apathetic sort of "stale" love. You could have had some combination of father figures—maybe a surrogate type of father who was a family friend, an uncle, coach, or grandfather. In any case, this relationship has shaped the way you understand love. (More on this subject in a later chapter.)

The impact of our father figures (or lack thereof) is only the beginning. Other types of relationships form our experience and expectations around what love is, many of which are group relationships—like your nuclear family. If your family celebrated success and accomplishments, it is likely that you believe God is only pleased when you have twenty consecutive days of "quiet time," serve fifteen hours a week in some volunteer role, or offer some other consistently measured "achievement." If you grew up in an environment where conflict was avoided at all costs, it probably affects how often you confess to God about mistakes you make (and it may feed your belief that "punishment" is coming after every mistake).

Or maybe it's not family for you; maybe it's an "ex" in your life story. The way that relationship ended certainly impacted your next relationship choice, right? If the relationship ended well, you probably interpreted the next relationship as a new, exciting chance at love or a "fresh start." If the relationship ended badly, you were probably skeptical of others after such deep heartbreak. And if the breakup experience with your "ex" affects the way you view the next relationship, I can guarantee it is affecting your perspective and relationship with your heavenly Father.

To get a bit more personal on how this has played out in my own life, as a young girl, I equated achievement with love. So I spent quite a bit of my adult Christian life trying to impress God. I saw Him like my dad—meaning that I mistakenly thought I could show off my good behavior and hide the sin in my heart. I figured God was keeping score on my behavior and not my heart. It took me years for this lie to be exposed. I remember being a freshman in college when it dawned on me—I hadn't tithed in several months. This was totally out of character for me. Truthfully, I was waiting on God to cause my car to break down or *do* some other thing that would generate an expense equal to what I should have been tithing. You can clearly see my lack of grace orientation. When I realized

God doesn't love me based on my behavior, but somehow He loves me while knowing *everything* about me, my life changed. Although I have a new awareness of grace and the way God loves me, I am still working against my early ideas of love.

Here's another example. A friend of mine—let's call her Shawna—grew up bouncing between foster homes and ultimately aged out of a state system with no consistent sense of family. For her, love is not at all emotional or "felt." Love is provision. Love is safety. When she had a home, a bed, and food, she felt loved. As she is raising her daughter, she has had to constantly battle a tendency to perpetuate those ideas. Her daughter wants her time, wants conversations and "girl hangout days" to feel loved. Shawna thinks about her own life, in light of the current home and stability she provides for her daughter, and has a hard time understanding why her daughter doesn't feel deeply loved.

The examples are limitless with the way our experiences shape the way we define God's love. Sometimes those experiences can cause us to live in fear of abandonment and/or rejection. They can create a relationship with God that is performance based or one that is expecting God to be unreliable or unfaithful because that's all we've known. Don't get me wrong: **our experiences aren't the enemy. They are important aspects of our stories, and God certainly uses them for His glory.** It's not *wrong* that we've had the experiences we've had, and we don't need to act like they aren't real or valid to have a proper view of God. We can own the fact that we've gone through both good and bad human experiences just like the next person. **We have to be careful, however, that our**

personal human experiences don't become the *primary* influence on the way we define God's love.

Put shortly, my overall point is this: *we form our many ideas about love based on how people have loved us rather than how God has loved us.* Those flawed ideas become our personal compass for what we believe about love, how we expect God to love us, how we love others, and ultimately how we love God. Whether your experiences are negative or positive, or a mix of both, they have shaped the way you think about God and the way you engage with Him.

Have you thought about how you received love as a child? Have you grieved or mourned the loss of expectations that may not come to pass or relationships that have disappointed you?

As I said before, our experiences should inform our ideas but not be the sole, or even guiding, basis for what we believe. When those experiences become the compass, we end up believing the wrong things about love: for example, that love must be earned, or that love means loyalty even when our safety is threatened. When we start to measure love by how much another person fills the gaps in our personal experience, we have no chance of loving God (or experiencing *His* love for *us*) in the way in which He desires.

So, what's the solution to our second problem?

Solution 2: Define God's Love Based on Divine Experiences

Remember that friend I mentioned a few paragraphs back who bounced between foster homes for almost the entirety of her childhood? One day she and I were in a conversation about her amazing life journey, and she shared a story with me that pretty much left my jaw on the floor but also reminded me of God's constant presence in our lives even before we choose Him.

She told me of a time when she was on the streets and alone as a young teenager trying to fend for herself in one of the busiest cities in the nation. She found herself sleeping in a stairwell, and while she slept, she heard a voice call her name with urgency. She jolted awake and heard nothing but silence. As she's telling me the story, she says that the silence is actually what startled her. She had never heard silence in those busy downtown streets. She jumped up and something told her to move. She walked to the bottom of the stairs and out of that building. And after she got about twenty or thirty feet away, she heard an explosion of gunfire. What she later learned was that two rival gangs were having a shoot-out in that stairwell. One gang was coming from the top of the building down the stairs and another gang was coming from the ground up the stairs; they met where she was sleeping.

If she had stayed where she was sleeping, her life would have ended without question. Note, this encounter happened before she had surrendered her life to God. When she tells me about that situation and many others, she confirms what Christians believe to be true about God. That He gives us divine experiences, shows us divine love, gives us divine protection, etc.—even before we commit to Him. I've never met a person who didn't have a story of God's divine hand before they said yes to Him. That means that even when our earthly father figures and earthly relationships disappoint us and skew our understanding of love, there has always been a present God giving us glimpses of something different. So, if we're going to love the way God calls us to, we have to lean fully into the divine experiences we've had rather than the earthly ones. Remember, we don't discard the earthly experiences—they have value. They shape us, build testimony, stir passions, and on and on. But they must come in second to the divine experiences when it comes to shaping what we believe about love and how we give it.

Problem 3—A Natural Approach to an Unnatural Love

One night I was helping my eleven-year-old son complete the challenging task of middle-school math. He was getting discouraged because multiplying and dividing improper fractions is probably one of his least favorite activities. He was vocal in letting me know how hard all of this was to the point where it was sounding like self-defeat. So I spoke to him for a few minutes and shared with him the challenges I had in school. He was surprised. But I told him that a lot of things that are worth our time and effort aren't necessarily easy. We don't finish fifth-grade math in one night. We don't graduate from high school with just a few minutes of dedication. On and on through college, career, or whatever else we may pursue in life. He argued that soccer and building Legos were easy activities for him—they came naturally due to his personality and natural wiring. He argued that he could clearly be good at things without too much effort. Nothing like deep disagreement with your eleven-year-old.

To help him connect the dots, I asked my son if he still had to work hard at soccer practice, or was he naturally the best in every game without any effort? I asked him if he still had to stop to think, plan, and search for the perfect piece when he's creating Legos, or do they just build themselves with little to no work? He finally began to understand that most things in life don't come easy. And even in the case that something does come a little more naturally to us, it's still going to require hard work along the way.

Don't we all make this same mistake when it comes to love? Many times we think love should be easy. Or we assume we should only lean into the demands of love that line up with our personality type so that it feels more natural to us. Many of us have convinced ourselves that love in friendships, romantic relationships, or family should feel natural or align with our natural temperament, and if it requires too much work, it's not always worth the effort.

Consider your own personality and things that come naturally to you. Are you a person who's driven to accomplish or achieve? Are you detail oriented? Do you prefer loyalty to a few friends, or are you energized by crowds? These questions are necessary to consider because your temperament matters. No matter the result of any sort of personality test you've taken, rest assured that your personality definitely shapes not only your perspective on love but also which requirements of love you're willing to meet.

Here's an example. Let's say a friend or colleague comes to you with complaints about another person. The venting session begins to journey toward gossip and overall lack of kindness toward the person. You start to feel uncomfortable and realize that the Holy Spirit is prompting you to practice love in a specific way: to stop the conversation because it is now unhealthy, unproductive, and unkind. If you have a personality that values keeping the peace, you may ignore that prompting, allowing this conversation to continue. Your inner turmoil may intensify, but you are afraid to upset your friend or sound unsympathetic. Unsure of what to do, you stay silent. Maybe after you leave your friend, the thought that you need to challenge what was said won't leave your mind, but the fear of damaging the relationship takes precedence. You may wrestle with this for hours or even days.

On the other hand, if your personality is direct or confrontational in this scenario (that would be me), and you feel the pull of the Spirit to practice love by stopping the gossip, you might be naturally inclined to quickly interrupt your friend and shut down the conversation. Maybe you also sharply challenge your friend with Ephesians 4:29, where Paul writes: "Do not let any unwholesome talk come out of your mouths" (NIV), and refuse to let your friend respond. Perhaps you even avoid her for a while after the conversation, making her feel like you're giving her the cold shoulder. While your ultimate aim is admirable in your diligence to avoid negative talk, you may not realize you have disregarded your friend's feelings altogether, or silenced what she would have said in response. If you are a self-proclaimed "truth teller" or "tough love giver," this might describe you. Your desire to be right and address problems can quickly take such priority that your relationships may suffer, as you struggle to give grace and to correct others in a spirit of gentleness rather than harshness.

Here's one more scenario. What happens when someone betrays your trust? Whether a friend, spouse, child, coworker, or parent—it hurts. What strategy feels most natural to you? Do you need to "get to the bottom of it" by accumulating facts and details so it can be discussed at length? Do you require an apology or acknowledgment? Do you withdraw? Most importantly, are you able to love after that betrayal? People who place a high value on loyalty—or have strict views of justice—will struggle with unforgiveness in the face of offense if they don't purposefully work against their nature. Without awareness and countermeasures, they will offer a restricted love that reminds the other person that they owe a debt. Have you ever been in a relationship (friendship, family, or romantic) where there is a debt-debtor dynamic? Whether you're the one in debt or you are the one owed the debt, it's not healthy and it's certainly not enjoyable. To love someone fully as if they never offended you seems impossible. But I can tell you, it's not only possible—it's expected.

In all these cases and more, can you see how our natural tendencies can help or hurt our expression of love? **If we aren't careful, we can easily slip into only pursuing the parts of loving others that come naturally to us.** But that's a problem because love requires certain things that will never come naturally. The way God loves us—and the way He expects us to love others—will feel unnatural and sometimes impossible. It will grate against our personality. There will be times we're called to confront someone in love though our personality is naturally more timid. On the flip side, there might be times we're called to let love mercifully cover someone's mistake without making a fuss over it, while our personality would rather be more confrontational. It's unwise to take a natural approach to an unnatural—make that *super*natural—love. Our own natural inclinations and abilities will eventually fail us.

When God's standard of love requires you to do something outside of your natural inclinations or personality type, can you pursue it anyway? It will require you to stop putting your trust in what comes natural but rather "lean in" to the supernatural expression of love you have been empowered by God to display. This is not to say your bent toward loyalty and harmony or confrontation and truth is bad. Your attributes are wonderfully unique and necessary to God's plan for your life. But if you are not intentional about recognizing when those good things get in the way of divine love, you'll find yourself in a personality pitfall.

Solution 3: Love from a Supernatural Place of Protection

When loving someone else God's way feels as unnatural as humanly possible, it should send us back to the supernatural nature of God's love. And what can we observe about this supernatural love? While the world always waits for the other person to do what's right, the divine love of God makes the first move. The Greek word for divine love—*agape*—describes that kind of love (more on *agape* later; it's powerful stuff). Consider these verses that show us the order of events when it comes to love:

- Romans 5:8 (ESV): "But God shows his love for us in that while we were still sinners, Christ died for us." See how God chose to send his Son to die for us while we were still sinners? He didn't wait for us to make the first move. He made it. That's supernatural love compared to the natural ways the world around us tends to love.

- 2 Corinthians 5:19 (ESV): "In Christ, God was reconciling the world to himself, not counting their trespasses against them." See how God's supernatural love releases offense before an apology or acknowledgment is received?

God has no need from His creation because He is self-existent and self-sufficient. His love for us doesn't add anything to Him. It is freely given as a gift, and He gives it *before* we even know about it or can attempt to reciprocate it. Just think about that. *God, whom we have all offended (Rom. 1:18), loves us before we love Him.*

Since we are dependent creatures who need God's care and God's world in order to survive (as opposed to being the self-sufficient Creator), we'll never be able to do this perfectly. We do have needs from creation—or more specifically, from our Creator. But here's the thing: the more we find our ultimate stability and safety in God instead of others, the more we'll be able to love others from a place of protection rather than from a need of protection. When we have no demands of people (that doesn't mean no *expectations*), we can love them freely. When we have God's approval, compassion, and faithfulness as the foundation of our lives, we don't ultimately need other people's validation, understanding, or even loyalty. Those things are important, of course, and it will hurt if someone takes those things away from us, *but it won't derail us.* Because God is the one providing all those deep needs. We're already **fully** protected and provided for *in* Him. Let that sink in. It means the way we love others doesn't need to be a means to secure those things; it starts being a way to let God's love flow through us to others *with no strings attached.* **That's a whole new way to love, right?** Repeat this to yourself:

> *In Christ, I have safety in God the Father that is unconditional.*

The psalmist puts it this way: "He who dwells in the shelter of the Most High will abide in the shadow of the Almighty" (Ps. 91:1 ESV). If you want to move away from natural love toward supernatural love, keep this

He loved me *first* so I can love others *freely*.

truth close to your heart: He loved me first so I can love others freely.

By now, it's clear to see how easy it is for us to be misguided in our understanding of love. There are so many false definitions of love in this world that we've been limited by, and so many problems with how we navigate it that require unexpected solutions. But we can address those limits one by one. We covered one limit in this chapter, but what about the other limits on the way we experience love? Let's jump into the next few chapters and see what else might be holding us back from experiencing the love God has for us and the new and surprising ways He's asking us to love those around us. Are you ready to go on that journey? I hope so, because it will not only challenge you the way it challenges me, it will change you.

Let's discover together.

Prayer: *Father, give me an open heart and mind when it comes to the way I define and experience love. Help me release the limited ways I've defined it in the past, and help me realize the power I have to adopt Your definition of love. Help me deeply experience how You have demonstrated and defined love. Take away my excuses, show me the path for healing, and prepare me to be open to the unexpected. You are wise. Your word is true. Your example is perfect. Your standard is undeniable. Your power is given. Your equipping is promised. Increase my awareness of You and my desire for You. And remove all the limits I've placed on my experience of Your love. In Jesus's name, amen.*

Chapter 2

LIMIT 2: Choosing Better Instead of Best

Conway and I had been married about seven years when I started praying for a baby. It seemed like we were behind "schedule" on the unspoken family-building timeline. In my mind, it was bad enough that we were still in our one-bedroom apartment. (Welcome to first-world problems.) I hadn't really settled or "nested" in because for the first five years of our marriage we were planning to relocate to Jamaica—Conway's home—to develop church leaders. We were living "light." And I was "suffering." Every time I saw home décor or furniture, I had to just look away with anguish. I knew I couldn't have it because we were minimizing what possessions we accumulated so we could move quickly when the time came. We were on the budget of an unemployed wife and a husband on a student visa who could only work part-time.

Around year seven the Lord clarified our mission. We decided to stay in the States and plant a church. And while this is being expressed in a couple of sentences, in reality, it was the culmination of months of planning, praying, doubt, and faith. The new ministry focus distracted me for a little while, but eventually my need for children resurfaced. I wanted to start a family and have five kids (including a set of twins—oh yeah, I was sticking to the plan laid out in my high school yearbook. Don't judge me.). Once I turned thirty, each birthday felt like I was getting further behind in the plan I had for my life. I wanted pregnancy, maternity photos, baby showers, and all the things that signified fruitful multiplication and normal family progression.

One day while driving, I had one of those moments that I later realized was divine. A young woman I was discipling at the time called and needed to talk. She was trying to break some unhealthy patterns specifically related to dating relationships. She called to explain a situation she found herself in. With confidence, my mind ran ahead of the conversation because I knew "how this was going to end." I knew she was about to explain how she had made the same decisions she'd made in the past and how she was currently experiencing the consequences of her actions. Except, she didn't. What she shared instead, with the sound of epiphany in her voice, is that she finally said no to a temptation that she had struggled with for years. She explained how hard the decision was and how free she felt for the first time in life.

Now why did God allow me to experience that conversation in the middle of my plea for pregnancy? Because He was showing me that my desire to "mother," though totally valid, could be fulfilled in more ways than I had considered. He revealed to me that what I really wanted was to impact the lives of people I had the privilege to pour into. Whether mentees, disciples, colleagues, friends, or my own children, I felt a divine sense of "rightness" when I invested in the lives of others. The message was clear. Although it wasn't in the way I wanted, in kingdom terms, *I was already mothering*.

I was frozen by this revelation.

It was bittersweet. **It was both an assurance of God's understanding of my deepest desires and an equal assurance of His ability to meet those desires as He saw fit. It was a relief and a release.** Relief that God was all-knowing and divinely loving. Release of my plan into the safe hands of my Father.

It was as if God was whispering, "You're putting limits on your idea of motherhood." I was beginning to see it more clearly. While parenting is of massive importance (if you're a mom or dad, I don't want to discount the level of work you're putting in!), God was making it clear for that particular season in my life, my heart's desire didn't need to be limited to parenting. I could experience the joy of nurturing, teaching, and connecting with the women God would continue to bring into my life.

In much the same way my idea of "mothering" expanded beyond biological motherhood, God's revelation of His love and expectation of how we love expands throughout the progression of Scripture. God's love itself doesn't grow or expand, because it is infinitely perfect and complete. However, God's *revelation* of His love to us and His command for us to love Him and love one another deepens and broadens throughout the story of the Bible. If we don't start with Him as the source, we'll limit God's divine love the way I limited the idea of motherhood.

Four Kinds of Love and Which One God Wants

Recalling our foundational passage from earlier, do you remember when Jesus sums up the greatest commandments of the Law in Mark 12? A law expert asks Jesus, "What is the most important Old Testament Law?" Here's how the response went:

> Jesus answered, "The most important is, 'Hear, O Israel: The Lord our God, the Lord is one. And you shall **love** *[agapao]* the Lord your God with all your heart and with all your soul and with all your mind and with all your strength.' The second is this: 'You shall **love** *[agapao]* your neighbor as yourself.' There is no other commandment greater than these." (Mark 12:29–31 ESV)

Where did Jesus get this? Why did Jesus immediately have this answer on the ready? Because it was part of His Hebrew Bible—more precisely, it was a key part of the Shema (a morning-and-evening Jewish prayer ritual based on Deut. 6; Lev. 19; and Num. 15). Jesus had been praying those words and reciting them since He was a boy—particularly these words from Old Testament Scripture:

> Listen, Israel: The LORD our God, the LORD is one. **Love *[ahab, pronounced ay-HAV]*** the LORD your God with all your heart, with all your soul, and with all your strength. (Deut. 6:4–5)

> Do not harbor hatred against your brother. . . . Do not take revenge or bear a grudge against members of your community, but **love *[ahab]*** your neighbor as yourself; I am the LORD. (Lev. 19:17–18)

In essence, Jesus takes these two key parts of the Shema and combines them to create a distilled answer to summarize the whole point of God's Law!

We can use the consistency of the past to help us know what God means by love in the present. We've already covered in chapter 1 that there are far too many definitions out there. So, *exactly* what kind of love is Jesus talking about here? Which Hebrew word for *love* is He using in particular? Because that tells us a lot about *exactly* what He expects of us.

There are two frequently used words for *love* in the Old Testament (*ahab* and *chesed*). In the portion of the original Old Testament Shema—where people were commanded to love the Lord with their heart, soul, and strength—the word used for love was *ahab*. You'll see it bolded in the passages above. That's the word Jesus would have read when He studied His Old Testament Scriptures.

Ahab has a broad meaning. It could be used to define affection for family (Gen. 22:2), friends (1 Sam. 18:1), or objects (Gen. 27:4). It could even be used to express intimate affection between husband and wife (Gen. 24:67). Finally, *ahab* was used to explain people's love toward God (Deut. 30:20) and God's love toward people (Deut. 23:5).

The second most frequently used word in the Old Testament for love is ***hesed (pronounce, KHEH-sed)***. *Hesed* is a covenantal, loyal love that God has toward people. Here are a couple of Old Testament references to God's *hesed*:

- "Though the mountains be shaken and the hills be removed, yet my unfailing **love** *[hesed]* for you will not be shaken nor my covenant of peace be removed," says the LORD, who has compassion on you. (Isa. 54:10 NIV)
- For no one is cast off by the Lord forever. Though he brings grief, he will show compassion, so great is his unfailing **love** *[hesed]*. (Lam. 3:31–32 NIV)

Hesed describes a sense of love and loyalty that inspires merciful and compassionate behavior toward another person. And get this: it is initiated *from* God *to* people—not *among* people. It denotes a persistent and unconditional tenderness, kindness, and mercy. In the Old Testament, God consistently seeks after mankind with love and mercy. Many biblical words such as *mercy, compassion, love, grace,* and *faithfulness* relate to the Hebrew word ***hesed***, but none of these completely convey the concept. **Hesed is not merely an emotion or feeling but involves action on behalf of someone who is in need.** *Hesed* expresses both God's loyalty to His covenant and His love for His people along with a faithfulness to keep His promises.

As we move into the New Testament, we see two additional expressions of love. The first is ***phileo***. It's mentioned twenty-five times in the New Testament in passages like Matthew 10:37 (ESV), when Jesus is explaining that following Him must take precedence over the way we love our family. ("Whoever *loves* father or mother more than me is not worthy of me, and whoever *loves* son or daughter more than me is not worthy of me.") And again, we see *phileo* when Peter is expressing his love to Jesus in John 21:15 (ESV): "When they had finished breakfast, Jesus said to Simon Peter, 'Simon, son of John, do you love me more than these?' He said to him, 'Yes, Lord; you know that I **love** you.'" *Phileo* means to be a friend or to be fond of an individual or an object. It's a love that is derived from personal attachment or sentiment. *Phileo* is a strong love, but still, it's not the love God expects from us.

The second expression of love in the New Testament is ***agape***. And here we come full circle because *agape* is the love Jesus calls us to when He states the greatest commandments in Mark 12:28–31, as seen in the passage above. *Agape* is the noun form of *agapao*. *Agapao* refers to the action-oriented divine love God gives us and commands we offer to others.

This is the love we should have for God and for our neighbor. This love is exactly the kind of love Jesus is commanding us to have toward God and others. While the other forms are fine—"better" than the world's types of love—this *agape* form is the highest and *best* one.

Agape speaks of a love that is awakened by a sense of value in an object that causes one to cherish it. It comes from a decision to consider an object or a person precious. And here's the thing that sets *agape* (love) apart from every other expression: *the quality of agape (love) is determined by the character of the one who loves, and not that of the object loved.* Put another way, even when the person you love isn't acting the way you want them to, *agape* (love) pushes on and sacrifices anyway because this kind of love is not based on the performance of the other person. It's based on the steadfastness of the one who loves. *Agape* is the most common translation of the Hebrew word *ahab*. This verb is used to express Jesus's love for us (Mark 10:21), our love for God (Mark 12:30), and God's love for Jesus (John 3:35).

> The quality of *agape* (love) is determined by the character of the one who loves, and not that of the object loved.

This type of love takes the ideas of *ahab* and *hesed* and adds another dimension. *Agape* from God differs from *hesed* in that it does not refer to a love already promised to a specific group of people. *Hesed* is certainly a powerful expression of God's love, but it was reserved for those in covenant with Him. *Agape* expresses the love God has for humanity in general as seen in John 3:16 (ESV): "For God so *loved* the **world**, that he gave his only Son, that whoever believes in him should not perish but have eternal life." *Agape* (love) is demonstrated in the greatest sacrifice—the death of Jesus who gave up His life as a payment for our sins. This *agape,* sacrificial love is demonstrated toward people who didn't earn it, whether or not they accept it. This love is for *whoever* believes. It's the epitome of a loving God constantly reaching out to all of His creation, constantly putting His divine love on display in order to invite His creation back to Him. J. I. Packer says it this way: "God's love is an exercise of his goodness toward individual sinners whereby, having identified himself with their welfare, he has given his Son to be their Savior, and now brings them to know and enjoy him in a covenant relationship."[1] Put simply, God now offers His *agape* (love) to all people, and it was epitomized in the gift of His Son to the world.

Witnessing a New Kind of Love

If you're wondering why this matters, stay with me. Because it does matter. In fact, this expanding revelation of God's love reminds me of an experience I once had.

There was a guy (like a big brother) I grew up with because our dads were best friends. He and his sisters and my sister and I spent a lot of time together because our parents were close and were committed to regular "hangout time" for our families. In many ways he was the big brother to four sisters instead of one. As we all got older, we kept in touch and stayed generally current on one another's lives.

We followed one another's educational pursuits, careers, and relationships. We had an easy familiarity that comes from years of close proximity. Then one day I learned some startling information about this familiar friend. I walked into a church I was visiting, and there he was. My "big brother," on stage, playing piano and singing. I was completely shocked. I stared, probably with my mouth open, in awe and surprise. I had known this person for as long as I could remember, and I had no idea he sang or played an instrument (and did both well, by the way).

After church was over, I found him, and before I said hello, I blurted, "What?! You sing *and* play?! Who *are* you?!" He just laughed and said, "Jada, I have been singing and playing since I was a kid." I wracked my brain trying to remember if I had ever seen him play an instrument or heard him sing in all our years of being around each other. I came up with nothing. Not one memory that helped me make sense of this moment. I was blown away by how well you think you know someone, and there still be so much that's unknown. That you can spend time with someone and know certain aspects of who they are in their lives and there could be things you're completely unaware of that have always been true about this person. This brings us back to the evolution of the revelation of God's love.

Remember, I'm not talking about the evolution of God's love—*because His love is perfect and complete, and it has always been that way.* I'm talking about the evolution of how He has *revealed* His love. It's like having my friend I've known my whole life and learning something new and unexpected.

I knew he was a great big brother, was an educator, and had a wife and two kids. I knew those things, but I had no idea he could play and sing. Watching him lead worship was an entirely new facet to my friend. In all that had been revealed about this friend, this facet wasn't new to him, but it was new to me.

When we think about *agape* (love), it is a new dimension, an altogether different facet of God's love. It's not new to Him—it's been there all along in His character—but as we see it unfold across the pages of Scripture, it's new to us. And it amazes us. When we start at the beginning of the Bible, we witness a God who loves *His* people, and then we keep going and discover there's more: a God who loves *all* people. Originally, we see a God who provides and protects those who *already* believe in Him in a miraculous way. In the life of Jesus, we see a God who performs miracles *in order that* people might believe in Him (John 20:30–31). Whew. Let that sink in. We have a Savior in Jesus who makes the ultimate sacrifice and then lets people decide if they want to accept Him.

I don't know where you are in your journey with God, but be encouraged by this: no matter how much you know, there's still so much more room to be amazed. To discover the unknown. To be blown away at the depths and facets of who God is and how much He truly loves you. And not with an ordinary love but with the highest form of love. When it comes to the kind of love He chose to lavish on you, He didn't choose give "better"; He gave *best*. He removed the limits of lesser kinds of love. He held nothing back.

So What?

So, how does knowing all these kinds of love impact us? How does it help us stop settling and experience God in the best way—in the fullness He intended for us? How does it change the way we love our neighbors? How does this knowledge make us less easily offended or quicker to forgive? How does it change the way we reply to an email or text? How does it change the way we see *all* people? Why does it matter?

Think of it this way. Imagine a husband and wife pursuing a better love than they grew up with. The two were madly in love at the start of their relationship, kept regular date nights on the calendar, and had a "no work past 5:00 p.m." rule in their household for at least two nights a week so they could focus on investing in each other and their children after the workday ended. But over the years, they let these commitments start slipping—particularly being done with work by 5:00 p.m. They both loved their jobs, so it started with a small change: "I'll just stay at the office late so I don't have to work at home after 5:00 p.m." But, at some point, one day turned into three. And then, at some other point, three days turned into four or five. It wasn't long before work became the one area of their life that was off-limits. The new unspoken law of their home became, "If something needs to be done for work, it gets done, no matter how many date nights or soccer games it costs." They had financial goals after all. It's easy to see that this relationship went from romance to roommates. Now let's say one of the spouses has an epiphany—a realization of what they've done to their marriage. What does *love* look like in this scenario? How do they love each other well?

Or picture two friends pursuing a better more mature love than they had as childhood playmates. They were once close and had a God-centered community connection that was important both personally and spiritually. But time has passed, careers have taken off, and life has happened. They barely talk unless it's about major life events. They both believe God is asking them to be more intentional, so they promise to intentionally connect at least twice a month. They have busy schedules, but they are tired of learning about each other's lives through social media posts. A couple of months pass with the same patterns. Then one friend texts the other and says, "Hey, I thought we were supposed to be connecting?" The second friend responds and says, "Yeah, I was waiting on you to reach out." They both go on to share how crazy their lives have been and start to realize that they are both having a hard time escaping the same old habits. What can they do?

In these stories, both the husband and wife and the two good friends are going to have to sacrifice a good way to love (work/busyness) for something more important (marriage/friendship). They don't need a better way to love—they need the best. The many kinds of love have their place, but they need *agape*—the kind of love that sacrifices—to save their relationship. They will need to be willing to discern what the other needs, make the first move, to be inconvenienced, and to take the risk of rejection. Can you imagine any relationship where both people are willing to "go first"? The relationships God wants for you require a love that lays down something precious to gain something even more precious. A love that recognizes *some things need to be sacrificed to give the relationship the honor it's due.* No other kind of love is going to restore their relationship to what it needs to be.

Hear this: God has done this for you too many times to count. His relationship with you is not casual. He's given sacrificially for you and me to be restored to Him. He made the first move. He kept His word. He has so lavishly displayed His *agape* toward us that we have no excuse not to understand (and respond) to the charge of the greatest commandment. How could we not feel compelled to make our best effort to respond in the same way toward Him and our neighbors?

This expanding understanding of love is the foundation for God's expectation of us. This is the kind of love God is interested in. It's the highest form of love, and it makes all the difference in your relationship with Him. *Agape* persuades the one who receives it to reciprocate it. We don't love God generically; we love Him specifically. Divine love shows us exactly what shape it should take and what actions it produces so that you know you're engaging it in it the right way. In short, *agape* opens your eyes to the ways you've been limiting your love for God, settling for better instead of best.

> *Agape* **persuades the one who receives it to reciprocate it.**

How might this play out in your relationship with God? What does *agape* look like on that random Tuesday night where you have to decide between time with God and binge-watching a show?

- Option 1 is acting too casual with God and minimizing the pull on your heart, assuming He'll understand that you'll get to Him later when you have more interest or time (something you might assume of your friendships *(phileo love)* when you feel like bailing on plans with them).
- Option 2 is remembering the kind of love God wants: the *agape* kind. The kind that is only possible when we lean into its source. The kind that is willing to give up a night of Netflix—or work or whatever else competes as top priority—to engage with Him as most important. The kind that remembers this relationship out-ranks all others and is far from casual.

It's in making those small choices of self-denial to pursue the best kind of love. Knowing that God not only gives *to* you but wants *from* you deep, committed, sacrificial love (*agape*) changes everything about how you display affection for Him. Not just on an ordinary Tuesday but every day.

Prayer: *Lord, open my heart to the overwhelming nature of Your divine love. Thank You for loving me this way. Thank You for Your patient revelation of this divine love. Give me a deep gratitude and high regard for Your love—the kind of love that is best instead of just better. May I never be entitled and always be in awe. Amen.*

Chapter 3

LIMIT 3: Choosing External Instead of Internal

So far we've explored two limits on our experience and expression of love. The first limit we discovered is the various misguided messages about love in our culture (and we learned that these are not the ways God wants us to love Him, nor are these the ways God loves us). The second limit is settling for what we think are "better" kinds of love instead of the best kind. This is our tendency—to set our standard for love instead of relying on God's standard. His standard is *agape*. So, how exactly do we *agapao* God? Remember, *agapao* is love in verb form. We remove yet another limit: we stop choosing *partial* love, and we start choosing *whole* love.

What do I mean? Well, let's consider some of the common ideas that come to mind when we think about loving God.

Does *agape* equal serving God? It depends. After all, you can serve someone and still not love them. Think of your physician. They can meet with you, talk about your body and your conditions ad nauseam, but they probably don't love you. They serve you with their time and skill during your appointment. But that service isn't attached to affection or devotion. The same is true for waitstaff at a restaurant, a salesperson in a store, or even the best educator in the classroom. They serve and provide, but do they *love* you? Unlikely.

Does *agape* look like singing to God, or about Him? Again, it depends. Think about it. You can sing with conviction and passion and still not love. Some of us have been brought to tears by our favorite love song, or from a personal anthem that speaks straight into a particular season in our lives. We've all seen (or participated) in concerts that stir passion in thousands of people. But we know that passion doesn't indicate love.

These same scenarios can quickly be changed if, for example, the physician is your lifelong friend or the song you're singing was written by someone you know. Suddenly, service and singing can reveal love. It all depends on the relationship. A fire in your heart, a deep bond and connection must be present in order for those actions to indicate authentic love.

A Love That's Already There

So *agape* is a love the Holy Spirit activates in the heart of the yielded believer, a divine love, which is expected by God from His creation, and yet, at the same time, it must be created by God in the first place. It's not something you can muster up. Remember from earlier chapters that the gospel—seeing how *God* first loved *us*—is the foundation of our love for God. We need the Spirit to open our eyes to see just how much God loves us and then empower us to love God back as He deserves and desires. The Holy Spirit is the bond creator. He is the love activator. The One who lights the fire of love in your heart for God.

When the Holy Spirit does this, it moves you beyond just talking about God, serving God, or singing to God just for appearances or to "check" off spiritual activities. Instead of doing those things to *earn* God's affection, the Holy Spirit helps you see that you *already have* His affection, and so now you do those things as an *expression* of love. As a *response* to His love.

Isn't that a breath of fresh air? Doesn't that take the pressure off? You don't have to serve God, sing to God, or talk about God to make Him happy with you. In Christ, He already looks upon you with favor because *you're standing on the track record of His Son*—not your own. When you see the breadth and depth of the Father's love, it makes you *want* to serve Him, *want* to sing to Him, and *want* to talk to Him—all as a response to the love He's already so generously given.

Beware the Pharisees

This is all such a departure from the way the Pharisees and scribes (the religious leaders in Jesus's day) understood love for God. In the days of Christ, those in the old-school spirit of law-keeping prided themselves on vast amounts of knowledge and demonstrating their religious behavior in front of others to gain external favor from their peers. In response to them, as in many other instances, Jesus flips their assumptions upside down. In Mark 12, He tells them their primary engagement and relationship with God must be one of love. And not just any kind of love. Not a casual love. Not a clinical love. Not a conditional or circumstantial love. Not an earning love. A love that goes beyond ceremony. It surpasses academic facts or mindless religious behavior. It refuses to attempt to manipulate others into affection—especially God. When they approach with a question in verse 28—"Which commandment is the most important of all?"—here's how Jesus answers. (I know we've talked about this already, but I'm putting it back in front of you as a reminder.)

> Jesus answered, "The most important is, 'Hear, O Israel: The Lord our God, the Lord is one. **And you shall love the Lord your God with all your heart and with all your soul and with all your mind and with all your strength.**' The second is this: '**You shall love your neighbor as yourself.**' There is no other commandment greater than these."
> (vv. 29–31 ESV)

Here's the irony: the religious leaders in Jesus's day would have certainly felt confident in their love of God. They thought they had this on lock. But their actual *lives* had already proven they loved tradition, public praise, and worldly position more than God. Imagine that—you think you're doing just fine in the "loving God" category, when in reality, deep down, you love so many other things more than Him. If that feels convicting to you, join the club.

Jesus makes it clear: that's not real love.

> Then Jesus said to the crowds and to his disciples, "The teachers of religious law and the Pharisees are the official interpreters of the law of Moses. So practice and obey whatever they tell you." (Matt. 23:1–3 NLT)

You may read that and conclude that it seems fair. Jesus is telling people to follow God's Word. In their day, that would be the law of Moses. For us, this would be the equivalent of following the teachings of the Bible. For Jesus to tell us to do this is a good thing. It's hard to find a better way to express love for God than following His Word. So, why are they not expressing true love here? Because while the religious leaders are *saying* and *teaching* the right thing, there's something else they've got really wrong. Jesus says it's wise to "be careful to do everything they *tell* you" (v. 3 NIV), but . . .

> ". . . don't do what they *do*, because they don't practice what they teach. They tie up heavy loads that are hard to carry and put them on people's shoulders, but they themselves aren't willing to lift a finger to move them." (Matt 23:3–4)

And there it is: they can teach the right things because they *know* God's Word, but they aren't doing the right thing because they aren't living God's Word. They're just teaching it and making other people follow it without following it themselves. Why? Because they don't really love God with their whole heart, soul, mind, and strength. Deep down, they love the admiration they receive by being *associated* with His Word. And isn't that the struggle we still face today? We have more Bible tools and resources available to us than we've ever had. We participate in church, we attend conferences, we scroll through endless sermon sound bites. We know so much *about* God, but how well do we really know God Himself? **We have become experts at spiritual display without spiritual depth.** Jesus cared about this in the lives of the Pharisees, and He cares about it in our lives today. He says their actual lives betray them. Their actions reveal what they really love, and it's not God. He warns His followers about this, and His warning is for us too. Look at what He says they actually love:

> **We have become experts at spiritual display without spiritual depth.**

"Do not be like the hypocrites, for they love to pray standing in the synagogues and on the street corners to be seen by others. . . . Everything they do is for show. On their arms they wear extra wide prayer boxes with Scripture verses inside, and they wear robes with extra long tassels. And they love to sit at the head table at banquets and in the seats of honor in the synagogues. **They love** to receive respectful greetings as they walk in the marketplaces, and to be called 'Rabbi.'" (Matt 6:5 NIV; Matt 23:5–7 NLT)

And Jesus doesn't stop there. After teaching His followers, He turns to the religious leaders themselves and pronounces a harsh rebuke toward them:

"Whoever exalts himself will be humbled, and whoever humbles himself will be exalted. "But woe to you, scribes and Pharisees, hypocrites! For you shut the kingdom of heaven in people's faces. For you neither enter yourselves nor allow those who would enter to go in." (Matt. 23:12–13 ESV)

Jesus goes on with several more warnings about their arrogant and inauthentic representation of love. Based on how these religious leaders enjoyed status and elevated themselves above others, it's unlikely they were having a "teachable moment." I don't think they were seeking to learn from Jesus. In fact, the Bible tells us straight up what they wanted when they entered the conversation with Jesus—to trap Him (Mark 12:13; Matt. 23:15, 18, 35). I wish I could have seen the look on their faces, or the glances they may have exchanged, when Jesus surprised them by stating the great commandment had nothing to do with a moral measurement or well-kept ritual and that their public displays of following it were all a lie.

What the Pharisees Got Wrong

In the end, what did the Pharisees and scribes get wrong? How did they fall short of the standard of *agape*? Let's look at Jesus's response to their overarching question, and then let's consider their failing:

> "'You shall love [*agapao*] the Lord your God with all your heart and with all your soul and with all your mind and with all your strength.' The second is this: 'You shall love [*agapao*] your neighbor as yourself.'" (Mark 12:30–31 ESV)

While the Pharisees seem to only love God with their behaviors and external activities, this verse makes clear that the whole intention of God's law was so that we might love Him with our *whole* being (heart, soul, mind, strength) and learn His heart for people. Jesus was shifting paradigms with this answer to the religious leaders. **In essence, He's helping us see that it's not about what you think you know *about* love; it's about the *motive* of your love and if you genuinely love in *action*.** Technically, these weren't new words. Jesus wasn't changing the law; He was revealing its full goal without rewriting it. The religious leaders were listening to words they knew but with the wrong intention.

So, how can we be different? How can we show divine love (agape) instead of self-centered love? Are you wondering if this pursuit is even possible? I have some good news for you: The greatest commandment not only instructs us on *what to do* but also on *how to do it*.

1. We Are to Love God with "All"

"With all your heart and with all your soul and with all your mind and with all your strength." How many times do you see the word *all*? Four. How many categories do you see? Four: heart, soul, mind, strength. *The whole you. Not parts of you.* Not just your activity, like the Pharisees did. God expects so much more than that. As a matter of fact, all of these have an internal source. He doesn't ask us to love God with all of our hours of activity. He's not asking for your partial love characterized by external busyness. He wants love that originates internally and expresses itself completely.

Why are we expected to love God with our heart, soul, mind, and strength? Easy: because *God* has not loved *us* with partial love. It's supremely complete. From 1 John 4:8 we know "God is love." Which, by the way, isn't saying that love itself is God. (This a twisted idolization, even deification, of the idea of love). This verse is telling us that God is the essence or epitome of love. That means His love toward us is *full, complete,* and *perfect.* Of course, our love toward Him is imperfect. Our hearts will always wrestle with divided devotions until heaven, but God doesn't lower the standard for us.

Even if it takes time and patience for you to keep giving God more of yourself over time, *He will never change His mind on wanting all of you.* And on the hard days, remember, divine love (*agape*) does not come naturally to us. Because of our fallen nature, we are incapable of producing that type of love on our own. And news flash: God already knows this about us. And He doesn't expect us to create it on our own. If we are to love as God loves, then we have to rely on His Spirit as our source. Romans 5:5 tells us, "God's love has been poured out into our hearts through the Holy Spirit, who has been given to us" (NIV). He expects us to pursue Him with all of our energy despite the inevitable errors we'll make along the way. *And* He doesn't leave us alone to pull off that expectation in our own strength; He gives us the internal power we need to pull it off. With this sort of empowerment, *agape* (love) is possible to offer God—we truly can give Him a sacrificial love.

2. Love God with "All Your Heart"

The heart is the reference to the center of our physical existence. It's the core of our identity and center of our human emotion—the hub of our thoughts and feelings. Remember this wording was found in the Shema so even in the Old Testament God commanded His people to love Him in a way that starts on the inside. The phrase "all your heart" means we are expected to love God from our humanity. Our physical existence is anchored in loving Him. Proverbs 3:3 tells us, "Let not steadfast love and faithfulness forsake you; bind them around your neck; write them on the tablet of your **heart**" (ESV). Proverbs 4:23 says, "Watch over your **heart** with all diligence, for from it flow the springs of life" (NASB). We guard our hearts and set boundaries so we can love God well. We protect our hearts to *preserve* our hearts for God alone. Guarding the heart certainly gives us wisdom in relationships and protects us from idolizing dreams and goals.

However, the main reason we "watch over our heart" is so it can be reserved for God.

3. Love God with "All Your Soul"

Loving God with our entire soul is as important as loving Him with our entire heart. The word for "soul" here is *psyche*—feelings, desires, and affections.[2] This goes beyond the human and physical existence we just mentioned regarding the word *heart* and speaks to the human spirit. It means "to be fond of God." To find delight in Him. Loving God is more than obedience and duty; it's emotional enjoyment. When we love God with all of our soul, we live like He is the greatest satisfaction. Is God alone truly what I desire above all else? It's so easy to focus on serving God without being satisfied in God. Notice I said *in* God, not *by* God. **This is a love that goes beyond what God does and finds contentment in who He is.** Only God can quench the thirst in every human soul. That's why in Psalm 42:1–2, the psalmist realizes, "As the deer pants for the water brooks, so my **soul** pants for You, God. My *soul* thirsts for God, for the living God" (NASB). Again, God doesn't just want part of you. He wants the whole you; it's the only path toward the fullness of *agape*.

4. Love God with "All Your Mind"

Loving God will all our minds means with our complete, intelligent understanding. The original word here is *dianoia* [dahy-uh-noi-uh] and conveys a person's way of thinking, understanding, intellect, and insight. Loving God this way is different from the affectionate love of the soul. This is intentionally directing your mind toward the character of God. Said another way, to love God with your mind means you regularly forsake what you *could* spend time thinking about and think intentionally about God instead. It also means the way you govern your thoughts starts to change. You don't think like the world anymore; rather, you think the way Christ does. This is affirmed in 1 Corinthians 2:16 when we are told we have been given the mentality of Christ.

Want to know how that change happens? Slow and steady. It may start with more time spent in prayer or study. Talking *to* God and learning *about* God are necessary to loving Him with all your mind. This truth has been essential to my journey as a Christ follower. It was so important that I wrote a book about it many years ago called *The Captive Mind*. Understanding the significance of our thinking is crucial as a Christian. Over time, as you continue to yield to the guidance of the Holy Spirit and invite His deeper inspection, you will start to see realignment in your mind. Different things consume your thoughts. Your career, marriage (or desire to be married), your money, your appearance, your happiness become increasingly less central to your thinking. Those thoughts are subjected to your thoughts of loving and pleasing God.

The person who loves God with the whole mind assumes this and simply makes *Him* the subject matter. The more we apply our minds to learn more *about* Him in the Scriptures, the more we start to think *like* Him in everyday life, reasoning according to His values and ways. Consider these passages that help you love God with your mind:

- In 2 Corinthians 10:5, Paul declares, "We are destroying arguments and all arrogance raised against the knowledge of God, and we are taking every *thought* captive to the obedience of Christ" (NASB).
- Romans 12:2 gives us another imperative regarding our minds: "Do not be conformed to this world, *but be transformed by the renewal of your mind,* that by testing you may discern what is the will of God, what is good and acceptable and perfect" (ESV).
- Philippians 4:8: "Whatever is true, whatever is noble, whatever is right, whatever is pure, whatever is lovely, whatever is admirable—if anything is excellent or praiseworthy—*think* about such things" (NIV).
- Colossians 3:2: "Set your *minds* on things above, not on earthly things" (NIV).

Aren't these encouraging? When we think rightly, we destroy the power of false ideas that used to take us down. When we love God with all our minds, renewal is inevitable. When we put our minds on the worthy things, we are elevating our thinking and saturating our minds with things that please God.

5. Love God with "All Your Strength"

"Strength" here is *ischus* and means "power, might, force, and ability."[3] This speaks to our *effort* in loving God. It's intentional, not accidental. Loving God this way means our bodily power and our will must be focused on loving Him fully. In the list above you'll see Romans 12:2. If you back up one verse and look at Romans 12:1, Paul says, "Present your **bodies** as a living sacrifice" (ESV). God not only wants your mind completely offered to Him so that it might be transformed; He also wants your effort. No relationship can be developed without effort. He wants you to work at loving Him fully but not in your own strength—with the strength of the Holy Spirit. God has already done His part in the relationship when He sent His Son to work on our behalf.

Jesus demonstrated His love in many ways including the effort of righteousness that His humanity demanded. Jesus was fully God and fully man, but the deity of Jesus didn't mean His life was easy. Our Savior was tempted by the devil and resisted. He pleaded for an assignment other than the cross but yielded Himself to the will of the Father. And *that*—the conscious choice and work it takes to yield to God no matter what—is strength. It's a beautiful picture of how we love God with our might and ability. It's Paul's charge in Ephesians 6:10 when he says, "Finally, be strong in the Lord and in the strength of His might" (NASB).

And guess what? The more we love Him with our heart and mind, the greater our ability to love Him. See how that works? This is more than "digging deeper" and "trying harder." This is about great surrender to receive greater strength. Do you see how God is constantly equipping us to do what He's asked of us? He truly is a good Father.

Think about your most important relationship. Maybe it's a spouse or a friend or a family member. They could say they love you internally, claiming they think about you all the time and have deep affection for you. But what if they never actually put effort into your relationship? What if it was all talk and no action? What if they never stopped by your house, never spent time with you, never showed up for you in a time of need, or never picked up the phone and called? They may say they love you with their lips, but their life doesn't provide any evidence.

The same goes for our relationship with God. Loving Him isn't always easy. We must consistently choose God over what satisfies us physically or emotionally, and when we do, we should expect the internal wrestling Paul speaks of in Romans 7:15–20. Don't let anyone tell you that loving God is effortless! It requires consistent work and effort. "*All* my strength" means I can't reserve my energy for crisis or for lesser loves.

Consider these passages to encourage you to love God and His ways with all your strength:

- "Let's *strive* to know the Lord." (Hosea 6:3)
- "*Make every effort* to supplement your faith with virtue." (2 Pet. 1:5 ESV)

- "As you are going with your adversary . . . *make an effort* to settle with him." (Luke 12:58)
- "*Make every effort* to enter through the narrow door, because I tell you, many will try to enter and won't be able." (Luke 13:24)
- "I always *strive* to have a clear conscience toward God and men." (Acts 24:16)
- "Walk worthy of the calling you have received, with all humility and gentleness, with patience, bearing with one another in love, *making every effort* to keep the unity of the Spirit through the bond of peace." (Eph. 4:1–3)
- "Not that I have already reached the goal or am already perfect, but I *make every effort* to take hold of it because I also have been taken hold of by Christ Jesus." (Phil. 3:12)
- "For this reason we *labor and strive*, because we have put our hope in the living God, who is the Savior of all people, especially of those who believe." (1 Tim. 4:10)

So we should love God with everything we care about, everything we crave, everything we think, and everything we do. *Our* entire existence is affirmed by the way we display that we love God. It's embodied in the words of Jesus in John 13:35: "By this all people will know that you are my disciples, if you have love for one another" (ESV). It's an understanding of the depth and breadth of the love we should have for God. **The love of God is the only love that *produces* love and the only love that *protects* what He loves.** When I love God with my *all*, I am bound to love what He loves with the same effort and commitment. It means I love His creation the way He loves it; I love people the way He loves them. More importantly, it establishes His love as the foundation of my identity and security like an anchor deep beneath the water that steadies the boat we see on the surface. This anchor allows me to love from a place of safety and stability (more on that later). *If we get "how" to love God, which is with our all and not just parts of ourselves, it gives us hope for loving others,* which we will get to in a coming chapter.

> The love of God is the only love that *produces* love and the only love that *protects* what He loves.

For now, I want you to focus on how you might be limiting your experience of God's love. Because your relationships with others aren't going to change into wholeness and fullness until your relationship with God is changed first. Which part of yourself are you holding back from Him? In what ways might you be choosing *external* instead of *internal*? *Partial* instead of *whole*? If you want to experience a love that isn't limited, you must give your all, and it starts on the inside then works its way out.

Prayer: *Lord, thank You for how You love me. I will never comprehend the height and depth of Your divine love. Lord, help me love You with my entire being—with my physical being, with my thoughts, with my affections, and with my ability. Show me where I struggle to love You fully, and then lead me in the new way. Thank You for Your kindness, for Your patience, and for Your divine love. In Jesus's name, amen.*

Chapter 4

LIMIT 4: Trying to Give Before You Receive

I was born and raised in Texas, so I am no stranger to hot summers. In our five months of summer (yes, FIVE), triple-digit temperatures are to be expected. With those high temperatures can come strict city restrictions on water use in order to protect our resources. They may add time restrictions on what time of day, or what days of the week, you can water your yard. We have even hit such low water levels that cities completely banned businesses from watering any grass on their property. We don't need to ask why—it's obvious. You can't give what you don't have. If you deplete your source, you have nothing to give.

And yet that's what many of us do with love, isn't it? The fourth limit to explore in our experience with love is exactly this: trying to give *agape* (love) before we receive it firsthand, from its source.

You likely already know God is the source of this love. The natural question, then, becomes, "Okay, so how do I receive it from Him?"

First, you have to acknowledge that He is not an impersonal force or a detached deity. He's a *person*. And not just any type of person. He's a *Father*. You might need to consider whether you fully receive love from your Father in heaven. If not, you will limit the way you love Him. It may all stem from the way you received love (or rejection) from your earthly father. I mentioned this briefly in the opening chapter, but let's dive deeper.

The Role of a Father

In the Old Testament, the head of every family or tribe was a father. It was a strongly patriarchal family structure. The role of the patriarch was to care for his tribe. Should someone end up on the outskirts of his tribe, it was his job to put his own resources on the line to ransom this family member who had been driven to the margins of society by poverty, or seized by an enemy against whom he had no defense, or enslaved by the consequences of a faithless life.[4] Now, for the record, the idea of patriarchy is a touchy subject these days. There are voices in our society today that have equated the word with oppression and misogyny, and given the way some men have treated others, I can understand why. But God's original intention in Israel's society was for the father to create a safety net for the entire tribe, and much of Scripture is to be read through the lens of a father who protects and provides with love and ability. With goodwill and sovereignty.

When we look at God as Father, we see that Jehovah is the ultimate Redeemer of lost "family" members. When the Bible talks about God seeking and saving the lost, it is presenting God as the father of the clan who has announced His intent to redeem His lost family members. Scholar Sandra Richter says it this way: "Not only has he agreed to pay whatever ransom is required, but he has sent the most cherished member of his household to accomplish his intent—his firstborn son."[5] This is why in the family of God we are brothers and sisters and why God is our Father. We are connected to Him as sons and daughters of a loving Father (Rom. 8:16; 2 Cor. 6:18). *That's* how He wants us to understand Him. The one who will put everything on the line to keep us safe and who will come after us if we get lost or enter dangerous territory.

God's design for a father in Israel's culture was to be a protector, provider, and priest (spiritual shepherd), and that design is upheld by Jesus during His time on earth.

Declaring God as Father was integral to Jesus's ministry. He calls God "Father" well over 150 times in the Scripture. In John 8, Jesus has an exchange with the hypocritical religious leaders of the day. They were angry when He declared that God is His Father. They stuck to the letter of the law and said Abraham was their Father. Jesus shut them down completely in a brilliant reply when He said, "If you were Abraham's children, you would be doing the works Abraham did" (John 8:39 ESV). He was basically telling them that if they had any understanding of being fathered, they would understand this new revelation of God as Father. Whoa. Just whoa, Jesus! On top of that, when Jesus taught us to pray the Lord's Prayer—the most famous prayer in history—He begins it with "Our Father." There's no getting around it—the kind of love (*agape*) we are supposed to receive in this life is only realized when we see God as Father.

But "supposed to receive" and "actually receive" are two different things. The question is not whether this love has been given by God. It's whether you have made the choice to receive it. If you didn't receive healthy affirmation from your father, or father figure, you can guarantee you will have a father wound. We were designed to be affirmed by a father, but tragically, many of us were not. Every single one of us can say that our experience with an earthly father has fallen short of perfection. Even the best of dads fails sometimes. And given those failures, you and I have both been left with some type of father wound. Whether you have minor scrapes or a deep cut that requires a longer healing process, your ability to see God as Father, love God as Father, and love the way the Father wants you to love will be affected.

> **If you didn't receive healthy affirmation from your father, or father figure, you can guarantee you will have a father wound.**

If your father was angry, passive, absent, apathetic, performance driven, or emotionally unavailable, you're affected. We were designed for love, so we tend to make the necessary adjustments (even as children) to get that love—even if it's unhealthy. The challenge is that those adjustments become the "bible" for the way we approach life and our connection to God. If you grew up worried about an angry father, the way you express love might be based on a need for peace and safety. If you had a passive or absent father, the way you express love may be driven by a need to be approved or to avoid abandonment. There are so many experience-driven versions of love that one book couldn't cover them all. That's not my goal here. My goal is to make sure you don't overlook the impact of your "father experience" on *how* you understand and receive love from God and *how* you are able to love Him in return.

If it feels frightening to think through this in your own life, I'll go first and tell you how this has impacted me. There was a time in my life when people kept giving me the same feedback about how I interacted in relationships: I always had an excuse. Not just an excuse but a *defense*. I said things like: "I'm sorry you took it that way" (the worst form of apology ever). I spent time explaining who I was so the person wouldn't be offended by my harsh words, my abruptness, or my low level of empathy. "Everybody is wired differently. It's not personal. I'm task oriented." Technically, all of these things were true, but in that context, the truth became a wall that kept me from loving well.

As the words of Philippians 2:3 (ESV) ("in humility count others more significant than yourselves") penetrated my heart, my thinking began to shift. God spoke to my spirit and showed me how I was attempting to separate my love for God from my love for people. My father wound—a constant need for approval through achievement—started to get in my way. (This is not to blame my father but to acknowledge ever-present imperfections in our humanity.) When I encountered people who were trying to express how my actions or words had hurt them; I saw that as failure. And that was *not* okay with me. I couldn't fail, so I had to figure out a way for it not to be my fault. It was like my "pass" that excused me from empathy, accountability, and humility. What a wreck. I hadn't dealt with my father wounds. I was trying to give love, but it was clear I wasn't receiving it fully. Not in the way God wanted me to. I hadn't let the Word of God and my love for God consume me; rather, I had limited it to certain compartments of my life. I wasn't choosing to put myself in someone else's shoes or make them "more significant" the way Jesus had for me.

My mindset began to shift, and is still shifting, from the defensiveness of "Hey, they just don't understand" to the openness of "How can I understand?" That took some work— the work of facing my father wounds and fully experiencing the *agape* of my heavenly Father. It's amazing—once you start receiving it, it pours out of you and onto others.

If your ability to give love hinges on your ability to receive it from God your Father, how does that work, exactly? If we were to move beyond the warm fuzzies and get specific, what does God's Fatherly love for you look like?

Get ready.

It looks like 1 Corinthians 13:4–7.

Fatherly Love on Display

Now, listen. Every time I hear 1 Corinthians 13:4–7 at a wedding, I cringe a little. Don't get me wrong. I love weddings and all that comes with the celebration of a new marriage. But when people choose that passage for their ceremony, they typically have a high form of romantic love (*eros*) in mind. Christians and non-Christians use the passage, so the intention behind its use is often not centered in God's love for us but rather people's love for each other.

This passage is so much more than a wedding poem or the content for beautiful wall art. This passage is a divine treatise of *agape* (love). So, when I was asked not too long ago to read it at a wedding, I asked for permission to explain it as well. I didn't want to communicate some kind of fantastical, whimsical emotion. I wanted to put this passage in a proper light and explain its priority in the life of the believer because it is the key to receiving the kind of fatherly love that changes you.

First, let's get a little context. First Corinthians 13 is the continuation of some teaching that started in chapter 12, which centered around spiritual gifts. In the city of Corinth, these spiritual gifts were creating major disunity and division in the church. The Corinthian Christians needed guidance on the purpose of the gifts, and it came in the form of a warning not to celebrate, or crave, one gift more than the other. They were clearly elevating the verbal and external gifts over other types of gifts. And then Paul launches into chapter 13. In the first three verses he gets right to the heart of the issue. Why all this talk of love in chapter 13, Paul? Because he's making the point that their problems with spiritual gifts are rooted in a lack of love. *None of this is about spiritual gifts in the end, he's saying, in essence. It's because you've prioritized giftedness over love. Who cares how gifted you are if you don't understand that love is our primary identity?* He dives deeper into the definition of divine love (*agape*) and paints a clear picture of it with these well-known (but often diluted) words:

> Love is patient and kind; love does not envy or boast; it is not arrogant or rude. It does not insist on its own way; it is not irritable or resentful; it does not rejoice at wrongdoing, but rejoices with the truth. Love bears all things, believes all things, hopes all things, endures all things. (1 Cor. 13:4–7 ESV)

This entire list is practical, not poetic or metaphorical. We should take it at face value. Like Galatians 5:22, where Paul gives us the fruit of the Spirit. It's descriptive rather than a directive. The list shows us what life looks like when we *are* led by the Spirit rather than *how* to be led by the Spirit. Similarly, despite several occurrences of the "be" verb, Paul isn't telling the Corinthian church *how* to be loving. He is telling them that when they are loving, these characteristics will be the evidence. It's not about *mandate* (You must do this!); it's about a *measurement*. (Here's how you will know you're loving well.)

These verses are a comprehensive look at God's love for us, and the Bible itself calls it *"an even better way"* when compared to the world's approach (1 Cor. 12:31). If you're wondering what your Heavenly Father's love looks like for you, here it is in black-and-white. Now some of these facets of love are challenges for us because we are created, dependent beings trying to claim what is only true about God. We need His love flowing through us, or it will be a distorted misrepresentation. (Keep reading; you'll see what I mean.)

God's perfect love is the kind of love you were created to receive. And when you receive it, you can then (and only then) pour it out into the lives of others. **Most of us look at this as a standard for how we love others—and it is. But it's *first* a description of how we are loved by God."** If we try to give it before receiving it, we are limiting not only our experience of being loved in this life but also our ability to love others.

Here's what that really means.

1. Love Is Patient: Paul begins with two positive aspects of love (*agape*) before he moves into a list of things that do not characterize *agape*. These first two descriptions will be longer because they are the bedrock of *agape* (divine love). The Greek word used here for "patient" means *"prolonged restraint, emotional calm or quietness, in the face of agitation, emotion or anger."* It also means *"not to lose heart and a willingness to wait for events rather than try to force them."*

Look at how God demonstrates it toward us: "The Lord is not slow to fulfill his promise as some count slowness, but is *patient* toward you, not wishing that any should perish, but that all should reach repentance" (2 Pet. 3:9 ESV). Think about how long He waits for us to choose Him and believe in His Son. Then He waits patiently for us to take baby steps of faith and slowly grow in our new identity as His children. He has waited, and continues to wait on us, longer than we could ever wait on someone else.

How many instances of God's patience can you think of right now? Probably too many to count. The idea of *prolonged* restraint in the face of agitation, emotion, or anger can feel unattainable. But if we focus on how God is patient with us, we can find hope. The patience of *agape* also shows up when one has the power (directly or indirectly) to get even or prove a point. Jesus certainly had countless opportunities to demonstrate His power and ability to accelerate a timeline (e.g., the disciples learning their lessons), but instead He demonstrated divine love. Remember, the evidence of divine love is the ability to suffer long. To endure unfavorable conditions with grace because that's exactly what God did (and does) for us.

2. Love Is Kind: The second positive attribute *agape* always expresses is kindness. The word for *kind* means *"to be useful or helpful; to seek out the needs of the other person in order to selflessly meet those needs without expectation of being repaid."* Now we see the synergy of this partnership. Patience holds back negative action, whereas kindness brings forward positive action. Kindness goes beyond the nice things we might naturally do or consider "acts of kindness" and genuinely seeks the Lord's guidance on how to meet the needs of others. Patience and kindness are often seen paired in the actions of God. In Romans 2:4, Paul reminds us that the kindness (generosity) and patience (restraint of God's wrath) of the Lord are meant to lead us to repentance.

I remember working on a ministry team at a church recently as we were planning for a huge event. There was a little bit of anxiety and quite a bit of organized chaos in the final hours. I really wanted to show our team some appreciation, so I started planning a team lunch to take place a few days after the event ended. In the midst of the planning happening in my head, the Lord prompted me to "go get them food now." I was like "Huh, Lord?" I was putting together a fun event with good food at an enjoyable location. We would make a half day of it, and it would be awesome. But I could almost hear God saying, "Girl, that's want you want." It's true. I love a party/social gathering with great food and great conversation. That would have been nice, but would it have been intentional *kindness*? Maybe. But I clearly had an opportunity to do something different—a chance to choose best over better—even inconvenience myself the tiniest bit. So I put the plans on pause and left immediately to get food for everyone. After I returned, we worked another half hour, and somebody stopped and yelled, "Hey, is there food anywhere?" It was an amazing feeling to be able to say, "Right here!" and start passing out the highly coveted sandwiches and salads. I felt a little wink from the Spirit as He whispered to me that this was His best expression of love for them in that moment. God will stretch us toward sacrificial kindness, which is more than giving out of our excess. He will call us to do things with a genuineness as if we were doing it for ourselves.

Patience without kindness can create emotional disconnection. Kindness without patience feels like self-centered righteousness or empty rule-following. Neither of those represents *agape*. In marrying these two distinct, but interdependent, characteristics of love, we can lay the foundation of what follows.

3. Love Does Not Envy: The word for *envy* here means *"to bubble over from getting too hot (boiling)."* It speaks to the notion of intent or desire. Jealousy is the root condition, and it's not new. It's been around since Genesis 4, when we are given the story of Cain and Abel, but it's just the starting point to derailing divine love.

When the resentment starts to bloom in our hearts and minds, it gives birth to envy. Envy takes the feeling of jealousy and decides to do something about it. Now, the Scriptures do refer to God as "jealous" in some places, but that is because only the true Creator can be dissatisfied when He is not properly worshipped or honored. For sinful humans, when we feel resentment, or threatened by the good things that come to someone else, we are living in a scarcity mentality and can't love generously. We first believe we're entitled to something; and, second, we believe God has limited resources, limited attention to give, or maybe limited knowledge or ability—He doesn't really know what's best. But when Jesus said He came to give us an abundant life (John 10:10), He wasn't just speaking of emotional and spiritual well-being like joy, peace, and inner prosperity. He was talking about a perspective for life. A mindset. If we don't fully grasp this, envy may destroy the work God is trying to do in us and through us.

Is this how you live on a daily basis? If not, you probably find yourself envious of others. Consider these questions in your relationships to evaluate: *How do you respond to the good fortune of others? If they do better than you, if they prosper when you don't, if their family seems happy while yours is torn apart, how will you react? If they achieve what you cannot, if they gain what you lack, if they win where you lose, then the truth will come out. Can you lose gracefully? Can you walk away from the contest without bitterness? Are you still assured of God's love for you and goodness toward you?*

These are the kinds of questions we can ask ourselves to check our jealousy and envy. This is the essence of contentment. As we learned before, God Himself loves us from perfect contentment and fulfillment. Jehovah, the self-existent, self-sufficient One, does not *need* us. Instead, He *wants* us and loves us from a place of total contentment. Our God wants us to love the same way—without jealousy and envy—from a position of complete satisfaction in Him. (By the way, when you read of God's jealousy in Scripture, it's an altogether different thing. He is jealous because of what is due to Him as the only true God. If you can't make that claim, you can never have a righteous jealousy.)

4. Love Does Not Boast and Is Not Arrogant: *Boast* means *"to talk with conceit or exhibit self-display."* Arrogance is a similar concept that communicates a person who is conceited. But when *agape* is displayed through us, it looks like the kind of love that creates a deep awareness that everything we have is a good gift from God. We often boast because of what we have created, achieved, or overcome.

But there is only one self-existent being, and that's God. Everything we've created, achieved, or overcome is because of Him. This awareness should protect us from the shallow, misguided antics of conceit. Jesus exposed people's behavior as inauthentic, dishonest, and self-centered. *Agape* doesn't try to prove itself. It's letting the truth speak for itself. It doesn't wear a sign exclaiming, "Look at me!" like the average toddler who always wants the attention and affirmation of others. When *agape* is flowing in us and through us, there's no need to brag. On the contrary, we give away praise and credit to God and others because we no longer need it the way we used to and because we are more aware of the truth.

Ultimately, **divine love doesn't have to brag because what's true will speak for itself.** When God talks about His character and His power, He's not bragging. He's informing. He is simply stating facts because He is self-sufficient, so everything came *from Himself.* On the contrary, when we boast in ourselves, it's not completely true because we are not the sole source of whatever we're bragging about. Whether it's God's air we breathe or a God-given opportunity we received, we don't have any reason to boast except in the Lord. Moreover, we believe in a Savior who *chose* to model humility as He embraced His temporary humanity. Jesus had the full power of God and was still selective as to when He displayed it. He let the truth stand for itself.

What would this look like? To be so aware of your dependence on God you feel uncomfortable with arrogance, bragging, or receiving too much credit? It looks like this: when a young married couple shares their struggles, love doesn't dismiss it as "young love" because you've been married thirty years. You understand you're only still married by the grace of God. Or when a student says school is hard, you don't have to talk about all your degrees or how you made it on your own with less resources—you understand you're only where you are because of God's providence. Remember, bragging separates, humility builds bridges.

5. Love Is Not Rude: Love doesn't act unbecomingly. Rudeness indicates defiance of social and moral standards, with resulting disgrace, embarrassment, and shame. It describes one who acts improperly or with intentional offensiveness and disrespect.

Think about our omnipotent (all-powerful) heavenly Father as the model. Although He's the one in authority over us, He does not use that authority in a way that is intended to disgrace us. God is not trying to embarrass us—even when He is correcting us. The Father's actions toward us are always motivated by love. He's always showing us how He loves *us* and how to love *Him.* He is the best Father we'll ever have.

We must also remember the example of Christ. As a Son, He respected His mother and father. As a teacher He honored His students (rebuking isn't the same as being rude). As a Shepherd, He corrected without belittling. In other words, love honors. Love considers the other person. Even as a parent, boss, or someone with authority we see that love doesn't need to diminish another to discipline or establish authority. You may struggle with tact, but love doesn't. And guess who determines what's tactful? The recipient of the words or actions. Colossians 4:6 says, "Let your speech always be gracious, seasoned with salt, so that you may know how you ought to answer each person" (ESV).

It may seem like too much to always know what to say. You won't get it right every time. Listen to the Spirit; He will lead you—remember He loves people more than you do. And when you mess up, *apologize*. The humility of love fosters self-awareness. That means we are asking God to show us our tendencies. And it means when someone is offended or points out an area in which you can grow, you receive it without defensiveness. **Love receives the offense and doesn't blame the offended one for being offended.** Love gives genuine apologies because that invites people to us. Be most focused on the relationship, not who's right. Even God did not call us to holiness before He called us to Himself.

6. *Love Does Not Insist on Its Own Way:* Do you have a friend who says she "doesn't care" where everyone decides to eat but then has an objection to every suggestion made? Do you know people who find adult ways to have tantrums when they don't get their way? Love doesn't react this way. We are expected to pursue selflessness, which requires a will to choose the interest of others over our own (Phil. 2:3).

Matthew 20:28 says about our Savior, "just as the Son of Man did not come to be served, but to serve, and to give his life as a ransom for many." Jesus could have insisted on His own way and dealt with those who rejected Him during His plea in the garden of Gethsemane, with those who mocked Him and against those who crucified Him. Jesus could have caused the cross to vanish in thin air or heal every wound on His body, but He was only set on doing the work of the Father. More important, can you believe God gives a *choice* in coming to Him? He could speak our compliance into existence, but instead the Father doesn't insist on His own way. He sent His Son so that we might *choose* Him. Even Jesus Himself invites us to know Him ("Come to me, all who labor and are heavy laden, and I will give you rest." Matt. 11:28 ESV).

Do you follow this model? Do you have the gift of persuasion, pouting, or punishing? If so, be careful. These can easily be ways you try to get your way or reveal your own inflexibility. Or perhaps you do it through charismatic, engaging, emotional displays in order to punish someone, or subtle sulking (when you say, "It's fine," but it's really not). Sometimes people may give in, or agree with you, just because you're too difficult to disagree with. **Not insisting on your own way means love yields, love collaborates, and love listens.**

7. Love Is Not Irritable or Resentful: This is telling us that love doesn't have wild mood swings or live in bitterness! Love doesn't make people walk around on eggshells and isn't easily offended. People shouldn't have to waste energy trying to manage our moods. I'm trying to teach my son this lesson. He is a big brother, and he's in a phase in which many things his little sister says or does irritate him instantly. "Mom! She's so annoying!" is the new phrase. She might sit too close to him, sing too loud, take a toy he's *not* playing with, or make a certain unwanted comment. She gets under his skin as only little sisters can, but I'm trying to teach him *that while he can't determine someone's actions, only he determines his responses to those actions.* The same should be true for us because we are so anchored in God that others cannot create that kind of disruption or irritation in us. When we are constantly being filled with a divine love like that, it starts to flow through us, and even the person who was once the most annoying friend in the world becomes someone who seems less irritating.

The other part to this phrase is: *agape (love) isn't resentful.* Another translation says it this way, "[Love] does not keep an account of a wrong suffered" (1 Cor. 13:5 NASB). In essence, in the highest form of love, there are no grudges. When it comes to our heavenly Father, the most obvious display of this is that once our record of sin is paid for by Christ, our Father destroys the account itself—nailing it to the cross, throwing it to the bottom of the sea, and remembering it no more (Col. 2:14; Mic. 7:19; Heb. 8:12). Said another way, God never goes searching in our past to accuse us of past sins that Jesus already paid for. God chooses to forget them entirely (Jer. 31:34). On top of this, when we observe the life of Christ, we notice that Jesus didn't hold a grudge against Peter's betrayal (John 21:5–17), and He didn't resent Martha for choosing busyness over being with Him (Luke 10:40–41). He didn't even hold a grudge against Judas; He just sorrowfully watched God the Father bring the consequences to Judas. If Jesus can let it go, surely we can too. So often we are hurt by hurt people with misguided intentions. Sometimes we think we have a malicious "Judas" in our lives, but usually it's just a sinful "Peter."

What about you? Do you find yourself scorekeeping in your relationships? In this new, *agape* way of loving, there's no more need for that. Choosing not to hold irritation or grudges in our hearts is the way we tell God we trust Him.

8. Love Does Not Rejoice at Wrongdoing but Rejoices with Truth: This is the aspect of love that gets overlooked when people try to paint love as purely an expression of acceptance, tolerance, and affirmation. That is a myopic, inaccurate view. Love has standards. Love wins when truth wins. Selfless love can't take delight in that which is offensive to God. To *rejoice in unrighteousness* is to justify it and make wrong appear to be right in the same way Israel turned God's righteousness upside down in Isaiah's day. We see a warning in Isaiah 5:20, "Woe to those who call evil good, and good evil; who substitute darkness for light and light for darkness; who substitute bitter for sweet and sweet for bitter!" (NASB). The prophet is warning against the lowering of our standards. Our culture, our fear of being "canceled," our relationships, and more can become a slippery slope for our standards. Love doesn't rewrite what God has said in order to be accepted by people. Love is how we adhere to the standard God has set.

Anything that is wrong in God's sight grieves a heart that is pursuing *agape*, not merely because the wrong hurts the one to whom it is done but especially because God is displeased with the wrong. Our heavenly Father has always been displeased with wrong (Ps. 5:4–5; Isa. 61:8; Prov. 6:16–19). Even as cultural values and standards shift, God does *not*! God has demonstrated throughout time that His standard of righteousness and His view of sin have not changed. He's provided different ways to reconcile His people back to Himself (animal sacrifices, ceremonies, laws, priests, etc.), but He never changed the standard.

Let's be careful not to alter the meaning of this. Although love is kind and overlooks the faults of others, it does not compromise the truth or take a soft view of sin. Love will sensitively confront and precisely correct because it cares deeply and knows that sin destroys. Rejoicing with truth means love gets excited when it hears of spiritual victories, and it encourages others by expressing joy over little evidence of growth. John, the apostle of love, wrote, "I have no greater joy than this, to hear of my children walking in the truth" (3 John 4 NASB).

When was the last time you encouraged someone with your observations of their growth? When you see someone respond in a more mature way, tell them. When you learn of someone taking steps toward forgiveness, tell them. When you witness someone's step of faith, tell them! Rejoice when the truth is taking root and bearing fruit—after all, your Father celebrates these things in you.

Paul closes this section with **"Love bears all things, believes all things, hopes all things, endures all things."**

9. Love Bears All Things: This means love is slow to expose; it conceals and covers (but is never in conflict with righteousness). Slow to expose doesn't mean lack of accountability. Rather, it indicates that love is safe. Love only tells whoever needs to know. Love has righteous intentions, and it rebukes in private rather than shame in public. God demonstrated this kind of love for Israel as He bore with the ebb and flow of their loyalty through the entire Old Testament and ultimately asked His Son to bear the sins of the world (Isa. 53:5). If He can bear with us *that* long, we can certainly bear with one another.

10. Love Believes All Things: Love sees the best in others or gives them the benefit of the doubt. Love is always choosing to believe the best about people, not the worst. This doesn't mean that to love is to accept everything that is stated as true, but where there is any element of doubt as to the real intention, love decides to regard it as good and honest. That belief shows up as an *expectation*. When I walk out to my car each morning and start it without a second thought, it is based on a belief that produced an expectation.

God in His divine sovereignty set expectations for us from the beginning. Despite our sinful nature, God has always expected obedience. In Exodus 20, He gives the Ten Commandments with the *expectation* that the people would obey. After the life and resurrection of Jesus, the Father *expects* that we will understand our sinful plight and choose to believe in His Son for eternal life. Further, throughout the New Testament the apostle Paul, the apostle Peter, and others *expect* that we want to live for God and therefore provide many guidelines for our spiritual growth (sanctification). *Agape* (love) believes or expects the best. God did it, and continues to do it, for us. What would it look like if you expected the best in someone? You might speak to who they can be and not just who they are. You just might create a divine expectation that invites them to respond to God and be changed forever.

11. Love Hopes All Things: Love has divine expectation. However dark the circumstances, love holds on to hope until all possibility has vanished. And even after the desired outcome is no longer feasible, love clings to the next best outcome, knowing that God is in control and good in His plans. This hope will extend to all things—to words, actions, and plans. Love hopes both for what is clearly stated and for what remains unstated because it delights in the virtue and happiness of others and will not credit anything to the contrary unless compelled to do so. If someone or something still has a chance to change for the better, love intercedes for it and holds out hope that change will happen.

> Even after the desired outcome is no longer feasible, love clings to the next best outcome, knowing that God is in control and good in His plans.

We cannot say that our heavenly Father hopes as humans do. After all, He knows what is to come, and He holds all power over the future in His hands! But His character gives us the power to hope. *He* is our assurance, His love fuels our human hope, and we are never put to shame (Rom. 5:5).

12. Love Endures All Things: Now we see that in the end love remains (1 Cor. 13:13). *Agape* (love) is a lasting love that perseveres and proves itself over time. The way we express that love, or act on it, may vary based on the health of the relationship, but even if love is expressed differently, it is not diminished. The parent who asks an adult child to leave home because of dangerous behaviors doesn't love the child less. The married couple that doesn't feel connected may not be "best friends" for a while, but they can still sacrificially love each other as they heal and grow. We need enduring love when romantic love and friendship love grow faint. Enduring love keeps the friendship alive when there's betrayal that needs to be addressed. It keeps the military spouse connected during times of deployment. It keeps a family together when someone has a chronic illness that shifts the family dynamic. Enduring love survives layoffs and promotions, successes and disappointments. It is tenacious. Enduring love rises above the visible circumstance to a place of invisible stability. This lasting love is in action when you "fall out of love" or "grow apart." *Agape* (love) remains after all the shallow affections have faded. It means the believer endures patiently and successfully rather than passively tolerating the circumstances of life.

Obviously, a love that supernaturally endures like this comes from God Himself, our heavenly Father. His love has endured with you unlike any other love has, and the same is true for me too. As Psalm 136 repeats *twenty-six times* just to make sure it really sinks in: "His steadfast love endures forever" (ESV). And He has the power to help that same faithful, consistent, enduring love flow through you to others. This can only be carried out by a believer who is filled with and strengthened by the Holy Spirit (Eph. 3:16; 5:18).

So, where does this leave us?

It should leave us speechless at the way God our heavenly Father loves us. In the gospel, through the work of His Son, our Father has been immeasurably patient and kind with us. And if He can be patient and kind with us through the gospel—when it mattered most—we can be that way with others, in both the big and the small things. He does not treat us with irritation or resentment. He offers us only truth, no lies. He bears with us, He is *for* us no matter what, infuses us with hope, and endures with us to the end. When you've received the full measure of this caring, nurturing, steadfast love from your Father, you now have the ability to pour that kind of love out on others.

But *receive* is the key word.

Have you received it? Have you dealt with your father wounds and run into the open arms of the heavenly Father who longs to fill you with all these things? You will be changed if you do, and you'll finally be able to love those around you with power and effectiveness. You'll be able to love like Him. To die to yourself in order that you might imitate Him. What a high calling. What a holy honor. What a worthy pursuit.

Come, receive the love of the Father, who has lavished His love on you better than any earthly father could. And watch what pours out of you.

Prayer: *Lord, You are Father and Creator. You are the Self-existent One, yet You love us so completely and so personally. Thank You, Lord, for a love that covers every angle, meets every need, and heals every wound, just as a Father's love should. Increase my capacity to receive this love. I know the more I receive, the more I can give. Help my unbelief where my faith is weak. I need to believe that on my worst day You are still kind and patient. I need to know that all of Your correction is driven by love. I need to learn how to walk with the humility of Jesus. Thank You for this sacred standard of love. Thank You for modeling it and lavishing it on me before You ask me to give it to others. Help me to spend my life pursuing it. In Jesus's name, amen.*

PART 2

Loving God and Others in a Whole New Way

Moving forward, let's review the main passage of this book (pulled from Mark 12:30–31 ESV):

> "You shall love the Lord your God with all your heart and with all your soul and with all your mind and with all your strength."

and

> "You shall love your neighbor as yourself."

We've covered the first part of that passage in part 1 of this book. We've explored what it takes to love God with our "all." And more importantly, we've explored all the ways God loves *us* first so we might be filled to pour out in love toward others. We've seen so many ways our love for God can be limited, and we've committed to minimizing those limits in our lives.

In this second part of the book, it's time to focus on that last part of the passage: "You shall love your neighbor as yourself."

What does it look like to fulfill this command in the power of God's Spirit, and *agapao* (*the verb meaning* "to love") not only God but others? Not just others in a generic sense but specifically with our frustrating coworkers, clueless roommates, disappointing friends, triggering family members, or even our enemies? As we think about the various neighbors in our lives, the remainder of this book will challenge you to love in these ways:

BE CURIOUS: Love Is Learning (Chapter 5)

BE FREE: Love Is Forgiving (Chapter 6)

BE BRAVE: Love Is Uncomfortable (Chapter 7)

BE RESILIENT: Love Is Unrelenting (Chapter 8)

BE REAL: Love Is Honest (Chapter 9)

Chapter 5

BE CURIOUS: Love Is Learning

It was a regular crazy day, and we were rushing to grab something quick to eat before we were off to our next activity. Probably someone's sport practice or maybe a meeting at church. I don't remember where we were going; I just remember that I was going to get Chick-fil-A for everybody to keep it simple, and that would be dinner for the night. I ordered for my kids, for my husband and myself, and I remember handing him his chicken sandwich, and he looked at me and asked, "Does this have pickles on it?" In deadpan I said, "Yes, this sandwich comes with pickles." Because you know sarcasm is my love language. He looked a little confused and paused, then said, "But remember I don't like pickles."

This was such devastating news to me. I could not imagine that after so many years of marriage (more than twenty) there were still some basic things I did not realize my husband didn't like. Maybe because we don't eat a lot of things with pickles, or maybe because I don't usually order sandwiches for him. It certainly could not be that I just had not paid attention. (I was convinced that this had to be information I had not been privy to before.) The revelation sent my mind spinning. And the questions started coming rapidly. I wanted to know if he liked pickles in general but just not on sandwiches. Did he like whole pickles but not sliced? Did he like sweet pickles? Relish? Despite the look on his face that expressed concern for my present state of mind, I was determined to understand everything he liked and disliked about pickles. It was my mission.

Since that day, he and I have had periodic moments, once every year or two, where we will learn something about each other that we are surprised we did not already know. It doesn't create frustration; it creates interest. That interest leads to understanding each other better, even in the small things; we can love one another more intimately. I mean, what's more intimate than picking pickles off someone's sandwich that was made by someone who wasn't in the "know"? Okay, it may not sound that deep, but it's the small things that create connection. Now I can simply say, "Can I have a number one without pickles?" If someone is getting a sandwich or burger for him, I can add, "Make sure it doesn't have pickles." It seems like such a small gesture, but for the person who must pick off the pickles from their sandwich, it could mean a lot. It certainly communicates that I care about every aspect of who my husband is, and I want to try to love him according to who he is.

In a similar turn of events, I learned that my mother doesn't like collard greens. Now, this is a particularly southern dish, and especially around holidays, we love our collard greens and maybe even mustard or turnip greens. I was so proud of preparing a pot of greens one Thanksgiving that I asked my mother and grandmother for their opinions on my first attempt. My grandmother said they were delicious, and I believed her because she does not give charitable compliments. But my mother said she didn't try any because she doesn't care for greens. I had a dumbfounded look on my face. How in the world did I not know my mother did not like greens?

Again, I had questions. I found out that she likes spinach, cabbage, and salad but not greens. I wanted to know how long she had not liked them. Was this a recent change? She assured me that she had never enjoyed the taste of them. So all of these years we've been having them at holiday meals, and she's never mentioned it. I remember just kind of staring at her like *who are you?* But like learning the new information about my husband, I was able to love my mother better. Now if I prepare that dish, I don't make as much, and I always make a secondary option. Usually cabbage or spinach. I know all of this may seem dramatic, but it's just another one of those moments when you really think you know everything about a person, and even the smallest piece of new information can catch you off guard. We often make these kinds of accommodations naturally for our kids, but when it comes to friends, family, spouses, and so on, the interest can fade. It may not seem monumental, but the person on the receiving end feels valued when they know they've been considered once new information has been shared.

Have you ever experienced that? Thinking you knew someone well only to discover some information about them that you were completely oblivious to? Or better yet, have you ever been on the receiving end of this? Having some sort of obvious preference that no one has picked up on for years and years? Not being noticed or seen? No one asking you a question about your life during a big event or gathering? It's sorrowful to walk away from deep exchanges with a loved one when they show absolutely no interest or curiosity about your life. When we are pursuing love according to God's standard, our love must always be learning. We need to have a curiosity about God, about ourselves, and about others.

In short, the first way to *agapao (love)* both God and those around you? BE CURIOUS.

Love Is Always Learning about *God*

You might be wondering if we really need to be curious about God to love Him. Doesn't He just command us to love Him and obey His commandments? Yes, He does, but He is not only a powerful God; He's also a *personal* God. In

> He is not only a *powerful* God; He's a *personal* God.

Exodus 20, as God is issuing the Ten Commandments to the children of Israel, on two different occasions He gives insight into *who* He is. Before He even issues the first commandment in verse 2, He says, "I am the LORD your God, who brought you out of the land of Egypt, out of the house of slavery" (ESV). The word *who* is personal. He makes a point to remind the people who He is and how He has delivered them. This is such a personal statement given the significance of the deliverance for the children of Israel from Egypt. Not that God needs to give us reasons we should obey Him, but here, in a fatherly statement, He reminds them that they know Him. He is the God "who." Again, in verse 5, after God gives the commandment forbidding the crafting of carved images, He reveals even more of Himself. He says that He is a jealous God and there are consequences for those who ignore His commandments, but there is love for those who keep His commandments. Even though these are directives, the indication is that they are driven by love. The love the people have for the God who delivered them is supposed to drive them to want to worship and obey Him.

Said another way, God doesn't want them to just follow blindly or because He has the power to make them. He wants His people to follow Him because they know exactly who He is and who He is *to them*. He wants to be chosen. Unlike other gods, He's the God who delivers, and He does it *before* He gives direction and requires obedience. He's the God who overcomes enemies. He's the God who makes covenants. He's the God who promised His people land and blessing. He's the God who rescues and saves. He's the God whose character does not shift or waver. He wants them to know exactly who they are following. And to know exactly who you're following, you have to *get* to know Him. You have to inquire and consult and watch. You have to learn. We do this with potential mates and potential friends—why not with God?

Since the beginning, God has invited us to know Him. To learn of Him. It demands an unquenchable curiosity. We should never be satisfied with what we currently know of God because the more we know Him, the more we love Him. In John 17:3, during Jesus's prayer, He says, "And this is eternal life, that they **know** you, the only true God, and Jesus Christ whom you have sent" (ESV).

The word *know* in this verse refers to an experiential knowing, not simply an intellectual understanding of facts about God or Jesus or the Bible. This need has led to many important works like *Experiencing God* by Henry Blackaby and *Knowing God* by J. I. Packer. There is a requirement for Christians to learn about this God they call "Lord." In truth, learning is a requirement for any healthy relationship. Even Jesus, in His humanity, "grew in wisdom and stature, and in favor" (Luke 2:52 NIV). God has made clear that He wants us to follow His commandments out of our connection to Him. Yes, we could obey in a disconnected, robotic way, but that hasn't ever been His desire. He wants to be sought out and known, and He promises that when we seek Him out, we will find more and more of Him. Just look at these places in Scripture where God invites us to learn of Him:

> "You will *seek me* and find me, when you seek
> me with all your heart." (Jer. 29:13 ESV)

"Take my yoke upon you, and *learn from me*, for I am gentle and lowly in heart, and you will find rest for your souls." (Matt. 11:29 ESV)

"Gather the people to me, that I may let them hear my words, so that they may *learn* to fear me all the days that they live on the earth, and that they may teach their children so." (Deut. 4:10 ESV)

"Let the wise hear and increase in *learning*, and the one who understands obtain guidance." (Prov. 1:5 ESV)

"It is written in the Prophets, 'And they will all be *taught by God.*' Everyone who has heard and *learned from the Father* comes to me." (John 6:45 ESV)

One thing have I asked of the Lord, that will I *seek, inquire* for, *and* [insistently] require: that I may dwell in the house of the Lord [in His presence] all the days of my life, to behold *and* gaze upon the beauty [the sweet attractiveness and the delightful loveliness] of the Lord and to **meditate, consider, *and inquire*** in His temple. (Ps. 27:4 AMPC)

How Do We Know God More?

God's Word

To know God more, we go straight to the place He has revealed Himself: His Word. We saturate ourselves in Scripture. We hang on His every word and learn what He has revealed about Himself in the story of humanity. To know God is to know His attributes, His nature, His plans, His heart, and His holiness. But more than academic understanding, we need applied insight. Curiosity about God makes us ask ourselves, "What does God have to say about this topic?" or "How has God spoken about what I'm thinking/feeling?"

This hunger to know God is more about investigating God's heart rather than creating a list of dos and don'ts. For example, think about needing to order food for someone. (Clearly, food examples are deep in my heart.) You're going to a restaurant this friend has never been to, and they tell you to just order something they would like. This friend can't tell you the specific entrée, but if you know his or her palate or preferences, you can order regardless of what the menu has to offer. You may know that curry is a favorite or anything with nuts is forbidden. You can take what you know about this person, even when specific guidance hasn't been given, and love . . . um . . . order well.

This same is true of our pursuit of God. We absolutely need application of truth. We read, we learn, and we take in truth so we can feed our souls and invite the Holy Spirit to give us His illumination. Jesus said the Holy Spirit would "teach you all things and bring to your remembrance all that

I have said to you" (John 14:26 ESV). This implies that we are storing up what Jesus has said. **We learn; the Holy Spirit sheds light. We absorb; He applies.** This illumination leads to life-changing application. But there will be times when the application seems out of reach or unclear. We won't find every life circumstance in Scripture, but when we pursue knowing God and His heart, we learn both His principles and preferences and can love Him well in our decisions.

God's World

Another way we can learn more about God is to intentionally observe the world He created. Creation sings of its Creator, and if we inspect it closely, we can observe things about God in His handiwork. Or, as Romans 1:20 puts it: "His invisible attributes, that is, his eternal power and divine nature, have been clearly seen since the creation of the world, being understood through what he has made."

Consider the sky. Did you know the heavens "declare the glory of God" (Ps. 19:1)? It "proclaims the work of his hands" (Ps. 19:1). In fact, Psalm 19 says that the heavens "communicate knowledge" about our Creator, if we'd only look up and learn (Ps. 19:2). They may not have audible words, but their existence bears witness to the character of our Father, and their "message" can be seen by "the whole earth"—"to the ends of the world" (Ps. 19:4). Some Psalms go even further, saying the heavens help us understand that God is *righteous*, that He is *judge*, and that He's a God of *wonders* (Ps. 50:6; 97:6; 89:5).

And it's not just the sky. Look at Job 12:7–10: "But ask the animals, and they will instruct you; ask the birds of the sky, and they will tell you. Or speak to the earth, and it will instruct you; let the fish of the sea inform you. Which of all these does not know that the hand of the LORD has done this? The life of every living thing is in his hand, as well as the breath of all humanity." Job's point is simple and clear: if you're wondering who governs all of life and has total control over the world, just observe a variety of animals and their habitats. Their existence testifies to certain attributes about Him—that He is an all-powerful giver and regulator of life. In short, another way to get to know God more is to look at the work of His hands: God's world helps us learn about Him. This is really important for the person who may not walk in a church or have familiarity with the Bible. God draws on people through His presence in the world.

God's People

Although people are flawed and imperfect, God still uses them to reveal Himself (and His instructions) to us. He uses people that are following Him faithfully, and He uses people who are new to the Christian journey. Throughout the Bible God spoke through prophets, priests, and faithful men and women to reveal His will and communicate His word to people. Today He still uses people to reveal His will. It may show up in an encounter with a stranger or in the middle of meaningful community. God will often send people to give a word of encouragement, wisdom, or sometimes

> **Although people are flawed and imperfect, God still uses them to reveal Himself to us.**

an unintentional nudge or affirmation to what He's doing in your life or what might be coming down the road. I know I have personally experienced this many times. Whether it's through a casual remark, an intentional conversation, or the unexplained insight of someone's prayer for you, God is always speaking through people, and it's up to us to listen.

Yes, God is inexhaustible. We are always learning, always absorbing, always curious. It's a journey that doesn't end until Jesus comes back. But it's not our only journey of learning and knowing. We take a similar path in our pursuit of understanding ourselves or growing in our self-awareness.

Love Is Always Learning about Self

Psalm 139 is a favorite of mine. In the first six verses, David has a powerful realization:

> O LORD, you have searched me and known
>   me!
> You know when I sit down and when I rise up;
>   you discern my thoughts from afar.
> You search out my path and my lying down
>   and are acquainted with all my ways.
> Even before a word is on my tongue,
>   behold, O LORD, you know it altogether.
> You hem me in, behind and before,
>   and lay your hand upon me.
> Such knowledge is too wonderful for me;
>   it is high; I cannot attain it. (ESV)

David declares the intimate knowledge God has about him, and he's simply overwhelmed by the intimacy. He makes the case that God *formed us, sees us, and knows us.* So it's really interesting at the end of the psalm, in the final two verses, when David begs,

> Search me, O God, and know my heart!
>   Try me and know my thoughts!
> And see if there be any grievous way in me,
>   and lead me in the way everlasting!
> (v. 23 ESV)

Clearly, David has firmly established that God knows him with an intimacy beyond his human capacity. When he invites God to search him, it's not because God needs to know him. This plea is so God can *show* David what He already knows about him. And note, David wants this self-awareness *before* he wants to be led in righteousness. He wants divine clarity about himself so he can know how to walk consistently with God. Curiosity about self in this way is not self-centered. It is God-centered. We gain knowledge about God, self, and neighbor as He tells us what is already true. Love seeks to truly understand.

So, how do we continue to learn about ourselves? The never-ending journey of self-awareness can manifest itself in several ways. Let me start with the simple approach.

1. Ask for Feedback: Have you ever observed some behavior or trait in another person and realized they were clueless about it? Has it been something that almost everyone else knew but the person in question was oblivious? It happens to the best of us.

Consider this example. A friend or spouse asks you a casual question, "Are you sure this is the movie you want to see, or are you going to change your mind after I buy the tickets?" They say it jokingly and with no intended offense. The question flows easily because they are convinced you already know this about yourself. But then the conversation goes from light to heavy. You reply, "What is that supposed to mean?" and instantly the friend is left to decide whether to (1) evade this question, (2) answer in your defense, or (3) answer honestly. Our response, and willingness to listen to the honest answer, will shape that conversation and probably conversations to come. If the friend is conflict-avoidant, she may quickly end the awkward moment and say it's going to be great. If she wants to be honest but is concerned about your feelings/response, she may come to your defense with, "I mean, you're a foodie, so if something is not right about a place, you want to go somewhere else. I get it. Anyway, we all change our minds." But if you and your friend have an honest relationship that is safe and invites regular feedback, she just might confess, "Well, sometimes we decide to do something and then you change your mind and either convince everyone to abandon the plan, or you withdraw out of frustration." She will wait for your reaction.

If you are convinced that you don't need to change or that she's incorrect in her assessment, you might shrug off her comment or go silent. But if you value the feedback, even if your feelings are hurt, you're going to be grateful for her honesty. You will say something like, "Oh really? I didn't think that was a pattern. I didn't know it bothered you or came across as self-centered. I just really don't like sitting through bad movies. Let me process that. Thanks for telling me." If you're *really* comfortable with these types of exchanges, you will ask more questions. "Does this happen often? How do you feel when I do that?"

Yeah, I know it sounds "therapyish." But people who want to learn about themselves—and are secure that they are loved by God regardless of what they learn—ask these kinds of questions.

After you leave your friend's presence, you would think about that a little more because you want to know the root of that behavior. You would invite God to search you. You would listen, learn, and start living differently because your sense of self-awareness had just gotten that much stronger. Can you imagine who you would be if you welcomed feedback regularly? Whether strangers or friends, people always provide a perspective about us that is different from what we think about ourselves.

And as a side note, feedback won't always be a lengthy conversation. Sometimes it's a quick remark or facial expression that gets your self-awareness cogs turning. It won't always be a beautifully packaged present from a loving friend. It won't always be delivered at the right time, with the right words, or the right *tone* (that's big for some of us). **But feedback is always, always, always a gift—regardless of the quality of the wrapping.** Make it a goal to know more about yourself than others do. Ask questions. Don't be quick to disagree, defend, or dismiss what you hear. Prayerfully take the pieces you need and learn, learn, learn.

2. Take a Personality Test: I am a sucker for a good assessment. I love assessments of our temperaments and strengths and motivations. And they are certainly not gospel truth, they are not 100 percent scientific facts, and they are not sacred like the Scriptures, but they can be useful on our journey of understanding who we are. Some good tests out there like DISC and Myers-Briggs perform objective assessment of how we have a tendency to think, make decisions, interact with people, and process emotion. I would suggest you take several and take them many times. When I lead discipleship groups, I encourage people to take temperament tests once every couple of years because life circumstances can change, and it takes work to figure out how much of you is "nature" and how much is "nurtured" by the life you've lived. The whole discovery process is fascinating. Don't be afraid. The good news is God already knows exactly who you are. He knows more about you than *you* know about you, and He still loves you, He still accepts you, and He still has a plan for you. Jump in.

3. Pray for God to Reveal and Convict: The beautiful sentiment at the end of Psalm 139 is David's invitation for the Lord to search him. He knows God doesn't really need to search him because God knows all things simultaneously and perfectly. But there is a choice that David makes to extend the invitation. Our God will never force His knowledge on you; He wants to be invited, and He wants you to respond to Him. So a simple prayer of asking God to show you who you are and what your next step of growth might be could be life-changing. God is so gracious. He won't give you a list of eighty-nine things that need to change by tomorrow. He will show you either an encouragement or a blind spot and the next right thing to do about it. You just need to ask for the faith and the courage to say yes.

4. *Review Old Journals:* I'm not sure you if you are a journaler, but it's never too late. Trust me, I am no model journaler. I am the person that has twelve different journals and planners in addition to twenty-four notepads, spirals, and Post-its that have random ideas and sometimes entire messages written in them. I would probably have to go through about thirty different things to get my whole story in one place. But I have learned this: when I write it down—*wherever* I write it down—I tend to remember it.

I have one book that recounts all the miraculous things God did for my husband and me during our church-planting years. Sometimes I flip through that book to see the "cheat sheet" of my own testimony and remember who God is and His faithfulness. That's basically what the Bible is. One big Spirit-inspired, God-breathed journal (with about forty different authors). The Bible didn't happen at the pace at which we read it. It was what God wanted captured so we might have one source to know who He is and who He wants us to be in light of that. You may not be huge on writing every single thing down in your daily life, but I challenge you to find a place to write down the big things God does in your heart and in your life. It will help you learn about God and about yourself, especially because we tend to forget God's goodness too quickly. Capture His activity in your life so you can see how He has moved throughout your life.

Love Is Always Learning about *Others*

Growing in our knowledge of God and self feeds our curiosity and compassion for others. Our journey in knowing and learning about people is not one of fascination or disconnected observation. People aren't exhibits. Every person we meet reminds us of our common bond in humanity. If we are observant, we will easily find common threads with every person we encounter. We laugh, we cry, we hurt, we love, we aspire, we regret, and we hope. The more comfortable I am with myself (imperfections and all), the easier it is for me to see myself in others and them in me. In truth, every person in the world is a member of one of our communities. Everyone is my neighbor in some way. They may be local or global. They may have frequent appearances in my life or show up in a one-time encounter. If you aren't convinced of that, always remember that all it takes is one pandemic to realize we are all connected and affected by common values.

When we are interested in learning what the Lord wants us to know about the people He brings across our path, we become curious like spiritual investigative journalists. We want to know the story behind the headline. There's so much power in a person's story. When we see beyond the surface of a person, we are compelled toward grace, understanding, and connection. Curiosity changes the way we engage with people. And remember, the command is to love God *and* people.

I remember a young woman I met and volunteered with; let's call her Jasmine. She was emotionally disconnected from our volunteer group. No matter how hard we tried, connection was difficult. Jasmine was friendly, had a lot of energy, and always made us laugh. But there would be certain times when she would suddenly disappear for weeks at a time. No callbacks. No responses to text. Nothing. I think we would call that "ghosting." What's interesting is that whenever she showed up to work with us, she was fully engaged. Even after two weeks of no response and no contact, Jasmine would walk in with her same cheery, hilarious self as if we had all just spoken the day before. When we would ask her how she's been, or why she hadn't returned our calls, she would shrug it off and say, "You know, life is life" or some similar trite comeback. We were all confused. This was more than an introverted personality. This was more than the busyness of life.

After a few months of this up-and-down cycle—a few weeks of showing up and a few weeks of disappearing—I invited Jasmine to lunch. I extended the invitation casually in the middle of a conversation. She didn't even see the invitation coming. She stuttered a reluctant yes, and we set a date. We met for lunch, and the conversation started with small talk but quickly moved to deeper topics. I asked her what brought her to Texas, and that was the thread that began to unravel her story. Over the next couple of hours, she worked backwards and told me about her current job, college life, high school, and childhood. Jasmine spoke nonchalantly about her mother who had more than seven boyfriends during her time at home. All but one was sexually abusive to her, starting at age five. Then her mother, carrying her own story, turned toward various substances to relieve her pain in addition to the never-ending flow of men.

The way Jasmine recounted her childhood reality was a total awakening. I had no idea what she had endured. She had learned how to emotionally retreat and disassociate herself from people in order to prevent pain. She moved often and avoided deep relationships. She had layers of mother and father wounds and had found a way to cope.

What I haven't mentioned is, when she wasn't volunteering with our team, she was an executive in a technology firm and a mentor to young girls. On the outside everything seemed like it was fine, but Jasmine was battling every day to stay positive, keep her sanity, not drown in negativity, and simply be the best version of herself. Talk about a game changer.

During that conversation I told Jasmine I was amazed at who she was and grateful to God for miraculously preserving her mind and spirit. That was a connecting moment I'll always be thankful for. It not only changed my understanding and interaction with Jasmine, but it was also defining for how I saw others. I made it a point to start to learn the stories of people, even if it was a glimpse or a slice, so I could lean toward grace and gratitude. And in instances when I would never know more than a passing hello or smile, I ask God for what I call "divine imagination." I would simply ask Him,

"What is that person's story?" If the exchange was too brief or with someone I would never see again, I would ask God to give me the "story" that would change my attitude. If I knew they had an unthinkable childhood, would I react the same way? If I learned they, or a loved one, had been diagnosed with a serious illness, would that change anything? You may think that's extreme, but the truth is—if **any** scenario would change my attitude, response, or expectations, I need to change them now—even without knowing the facts.

If you're wondering what happened to Jasmine, after that lunch, things changed. When I say "things," I mean *me*. I asked her if she would like to set up a rotating schedule of two weeks on and two weeks off. I told her it was because I understood the busyness of her life. It wasn't the time to tell her that I saw her behavior as self-protective and harmful to real connection. **We must earn the right to speak truth into other people's lives. We don't say everything we see. We wait until the Holy Spirit tells us the best way to love the other person.** One meaningful conversation didn't earn that right for me. I knew because Jasmine never asked for my thoughts or my input. This was her life, and she was figuring it out. So I gave *grace and space*. It's what we need a lot of times. No one will be pressured into spiritual or emotional health.

Over the following year, she and I had a few more conversations, and she finally asked me one day what I thought about her going to counseling again (she had tried before but it was a "bust" in her opinion). My little heart did a dance and fist pump because I knew the Lord was creating a small teachable moment. Praise God, I didn't attack her with a year's worth of Scriptures and devotional thoughts.

I calmly asked, "Would you prefer a Christian counselor?" I didn't want to assume, but I was saying, "Please say yes!" in my mind. She asked, "Do you think that's best?" In my mind I screamed, "Girl, YES! ABSOLUTELY. GOD IS ABOUT TO ALTER YOUR WHOLE LIFE!" But from my mouth I said, "I definitely recommend a Christian counselor, so the guidance can be Bible-based." I was really chill. I even surprised myself. I gave her a couple of recommendations and waited a few more months to ask if she had started. She said she had not. I said, "Okay. Whenever you're ready."

A couple more months passed, and she walked up to me and said, "Guess what?" Of course, I answered with eagerness, ready to hear the update. She went on for about thirty minutes telling me about her last five sessions with her new therapist, that she had no idea what she was suppressing just to survive each day, that she's starting to wonder if she has been self-sabotaging relationships, that she bought a few great books on family trauma, and that she's joined a life group at our church. I was out of breath just listening. It was great—as if God had opened a locked place in her heart and years of pain were being healed before my eyes. I remember thanking the Lord over and over again. *I was grateful that the Lord had given me curiosity to want to know her story before I held her accountable for her behavior.* I was grateful to Him for the patience to let her reveal her story to me and for the grace to walk with her until she was ready to adjust. I was thankful for her openness, my patience (which is truly supernatural if you know me), and God's work in both of us.

I now try to be intentional about checking in with God as I'm interacting with people or even thinking about them. Whether it's someone I'm having a conversation with, working alongside, or a cashier I think is moving too slow, if I had an exchange that was unpleasant or uncomfortable, before I get drawn into feeling offended or withdraw altogether, I often ask God for divine imagination so I can love well in that moment. I define *divine imagination* as "inviting God into our imaginations, or minds, to produce thoughts, feelings, sensations, emotions, or images." We all have imaginations, but when we ask God to guide our imaginations, we experience divine or Spirit-led imagination. It's the way a person comes up with ideas for how to provide unique hospitality, create a worship set, deliver a musical piece, or write great stories like The Chronicles of Narnia series and *The Screwtape Letters* as C. S. Lewis did. *God gives our minds dreams and/or experiences that enable us to love Him and people with unique insight.* It is evident in the poetry of the Psalms and Song of Solomon but also in the many metaphors of Paul. This shows up in my interactions with people because He may give me an idea of what their lives "could be like." Sometimes it's a discernment of what is true about their lives, but many times it's a thought, feeling, or idea about what *could be.*

For example, when the server at the restaurant seems inefficient, or unusually slow, sometimes the thought that comes to me is: *What if she's a single mom, this is her second job, and she won't see her kids until the morning?* Or the person with whom I don't seem to connect (and may secretly try to avoid), I hear, *What if he just found out his parent has a serious illness and he lives so far from them that he can't be there the way he wants to?* I know these seem specific, but that's exactly how it happens. I ask God to give me an idea or a scenario that would instantly change my countenance or attitude in that moment, and He does. Now sometimes I make them up on my own (imagination, people!). I'm not saying I hear thoughts with perfect precision, but the end goal is always to bring forth compassion, patience, understanding, or whatever I'm lacking at that particular time toward that particular person. There are even times when God has given me a divine thought that has led me to ask certain questions of the person or people that lead to divine conversations. Things I would have never known to ask. **Divine imagination stirs up healthy curiosity and forces us to anchor ourselves in the whispers of the Spirit's guidance when the volume of our feelings and biases is deafening.** I am constantly amazed by God's faithfulness to stretch my mind in an effort to stretch my heart.

So, how might you show *agape* (love) by learning more about others in your daily life? How can you be curious about others around you?

First, use your ***divine imagination*** to cultivate compassion in your heart for someone.

If that isn't your cup of tea, ***create a list of questions*** you keep in a note on your phone. If you're struggling to connect with someone, pull out that list and get to asking.

Third, *before you enter into any group event,* come up with three things you want to have learned about five people in that room before you leave—or something like that. Whatever it is, make it a specific goal so you walk away having learned about someone else.

Next, *after any social gathering,* whether it's four people or four hundred, follow up with at least two people with something like this: "I noticed tonight that you _____. I wanted to encourage you and let you know that _____." This is an easy way to make a charitable observation about a person and immediately encourage them about it.

Lastly, if you're really pressed for time and you feel stuck, here's an easy rule of conversation to get another person talking: start the majority of your sentences with the words *why, how, did you,* or *have you*. It will force a question out every time.

Choosing to be a student of God, of self, and of others is essential to growing our love. That curiosity fuels our invitation for God to search us and show us what is not like God. It stirs my appetite for self-awareness and, with the help of the Holy Spirit, allows me to see others as a collection of important stories rather than the sum of a moment or an experience.

Because *agape* (love) is curious, we are constantly amazed at the world around us. And in return, the world is often amazed by us. After all, think about how rare it is to meet a person who is truly curious in conversation instead of always using their words to prove themselves or shutting down completely? That would mean he/she is actually interested in people. That person would look for divine opportunities as often as possible. We all need to be more curious. In a world that's often disinterested in others unless it pays off for self, loving in a way that is truly curious is a whole new way to love God and those around you.

Prayer: *God, for the millions of stories we hold, help me see curiosity as a critical part of divine love. Show me how to ask questions and take interest with no ulterior motive so I can see clearly the people You put in my path and love them better. Amen.*

Chapter 6

BE FREE: Love Is Forgiving

When I was four years old, I found myself on top of a ten-speed bike flying down an alley behind our house. Whatever questions just popped into your mind after reading that sentence are legitimate. You're probably wondering *why* or *how* among other things. Here's the recap. I had a "big sister," who was actually our next-door neighbor, who was about six or seven years older than me. She had just gotten a new bike, and after watching her ride it a few times, I, in all of my four-year-old confidence, was convinced I could ride too. That, combined with her eleven-year-old wisdom, is how I ended up on her bicycle. We decided that if she could help me up and give the bike a push, I could coast down the hill. And this was in fact true. We did not account for the fact that my little legs couldn't reach the pedals, and my little hands couldn't reach the hand brakes. While I successfully kept my balance until I reached the bottom of the hill, I was unsuccessful at stopping. I had a head-on collision with some bushes and was pretty scratched up. As I began to stand up, I realized the metal bike pedal, with spiked edges, was wedged into my shin. (This was the late 70s, y'all; spiked pedals and no helmets were the norm.) That bike pedal left a serious gash in my shin that took weeks to completely heal.

Now, more than forty years later, there's still a scar to remind me of that day. It has faded over the years, but it will never completely be gone. That scar is a metaphor for forgiveness. It reminds me that forgiveness doesn't mean there's no scar, nor does it mean you've forgotten the story. **Forgiveness means that the story, not the scar, hurt anymore.** I can tell that story, as the Lord creates opportunity for His glory and others' encouragement. I can look at that scar, touch the scar, and talk about the scar without experiencing the pain behind the scar.

Forgiveness Demonstrated

In the Bible, forgiveness demonstrates two major ideas. The first one is the idea of giving or *granting* something. The second is the idea of *sending* something away or giving something up.

Granting

Let's look at Ephesians 4:32, which says, "Be kind to one another, tenderhearted, *forgiving* one another, as God in Christ forgave you" (ESV). The word translated as "forgiving" is the Greek word *charizomai*. It means "to do something pleasant or agreeable." In Scripture it is often translated as gave, freely give, canceled (as a form of benevolence), granted, and hand over (Luke 7:21; Luke 7:42; Acts 3:14).

Sending

Matthew 6:14–15 states, "For if you *forgive* others their trespasses, your heavenly Father will also *forgive* you, but if you do not *forgive* others their trespasses, neither will your Father *forgive* your trespasses" (ESV). Here a different Greek word, *aphiēmi,* is translated as "forgive." The literal breakdown of the word means "to separate and put in motion." In other passages it is translated as leave (most common), dismiss, or allow (Matt. 4:11; Matt. 19:14; Mark 4:36; Mark 10:4).

A couple things here:

1. As we think about how God relates to us, we can see that the Father is in the *granting* and *sending* business. When He forgives those who confess faith in Christ, He is both dismissing our sin and granting us unearned favor. Think about the depth of the Father's forgiveness. He "sent" our sin to His Son and granted us the righteousness of this Son. If you think on that for just a few moments, your soul will be filled with gratitude, awe, and joy. All praise to God for His extravagant forgiveness!

2. As we relate to God and people, here's what those two ideas have in common. First, both ideas are presented as matters of the heart. Meaning, there's no detailed behavioral instruction on what to say or when to say it or what specific action to take. Jesus is giving us instructions to understand the principle of forgiveness. Second, in both cases the instruction indicates a continuous present tense. You never stop forgiving. *You never hit a limit.* God doesn't hit a limit with us, and in turn, we don't hit a limit with one another. I know. It seems impossible. But it is truly possible when you're empowered by God's Spirit. He's the one forgiving *through* you; remember that. Also keep in mind all of these principles are foundational guidance for how we should think. Be careful not to dismiss them because of your unique situation. This is our starting point.

Where am I getting the whole "never hitting a limit" thing? This is clearly articulated when answering Peter's question in Matthew 18. Here's the question in verse 21 (ESV):

> Then Peter came up and said to him, "Lord,
> how often will my brother sin against me,
> and I forgive him? As many as seven times?"

When Peter asked how many times he should forgive a brother who sins against him, he probably thought he was being generous when he suggested seven times as the answer. But Jesus took it to an entirely different level (as he often did) when he responded this way in verse 22 (ESV):

> Jesus said to him, "I do not say to you seven
> times, but seventy-seven times."

Scholars say this could either mean seventy-seven (77) or seventy *times* seven (490). Now, this is not literal on the prescriptive level, meaning that Jesus is not saying count seventy-seven times or 490 times depending on how you want to interpret that. You don't get to hold a grudge at the seventy-eighth or four hundred ninety-first offense. Jesus is using the commonly known meaning of the number seven in the Hebrew mind, which communicates completion or totality. He's saying, *Take the most complete, total number you know, and just keep multiplying it.* That's how many times you should forgive—continuously.

You might be wondering: *How in the world is that even possible?* Surely there are some exceptions to the rule. How do we practically live in a continuous state of forgiveness?

What Forgiveness Is Not and Whom to Trust with It

Before we dive into how this applies in everyday life, let's be clear about what forgiveness is not. To begin with, forgiveness is not the absence of pain. It doesn't mean we begin to feel good about horrible things, and it doesn't take away the need for justice. But God is reminding us that *He* is perfectly just. *He* will handle whatever consequences need to be handed out. Those consequences will be handled divinely—and not always visibly—so we have to trust a God who understands justice better than we ever will. Consider the way Romans puts it:

> Bless those who persecute you; bless and do not curse them. Rejoice with those who rejoice, weep with those who weep. Live in harmony with one another. Do not be haughty, but associate with the lowly. Never be wise in your own sight. Repay no one

evil for evil, but give thought to do what is honorable in the sight of all. If possible, so far as it depends on you, live peaceably with all. Beloved, never avenge yourselves, but leave it to the wrath of God, for it is written, "Vengeance is mine, I will repay, says the Lord." To the contrary, "if your enemy is hungry, feed him; if he is thirsty, give him something to drink; for by so doing you will heap burning coals on his head." Do not be overcome by evil, but overcome evil with good. (12:14–21 ESV)

Or just look at the story of the persistent widow in Luke's Gospel:

[Jesus] said, "In a certain city there was a judge who neither feared God nor respected man. And there was a widow in that city who kept coming to him and saying, 'Give me justice against my adversary.' For a while he refused, but afterward he said to himself, 'Though I neither fear God nor respect man, yet because this widow keeps bothering me, I will give her justice, so that she will not beat me down by her continual coming.'" (Luke 18:2–5 ESV)

This widow is seeking justice, and in Jesus's story, even the world's most terrible, unrighteous judge was willing to work on her behalf to settle the score with her adversary. He is setting us up because if an *un*righteous judge was able to provide justice, how much more so will the only *righteous judge* do it for us even if it's through someone who does not love God? In the verses immediately after this, Jesus tells us exactly what our God will do regarding the things we desire justice for:

> "And will not God give justice to his elect,
> who cry to him day and night? Will he delay
> long over them? I tell you, he will give justice
> to them speedily. Nevertheless, when the Son
> of Man comes, will he find faith on earth?"
> (Luke 18:7–8 ESV)

Jesus is clear: the most righteous judge in the world will give justice to His children. He hears their cries. A time is coming when He will swiftly settle all scores. The question isn't whether He'll do it; it's whether He'll find faith in *us* when He gets here to do it. Will He find us right here, trusting and believing His justice is on the way? Or will He find that we got impatient and bored and took matters into our own hands?

God understands justice from a place of holiness and perfection; we understand it from a place of imperfection and pain. **In the end, our desire for fairness can't get in the way of our pursuit of forgiveness.**

Think about this.

The same Peter who was hoping for a limitation on our forgiveness later penned this

> In the end, our
> desire for fairness
> can't get in the
> way of our pursuit
> of forgiveness.

inspired truth about Christ Himself when he wrote in 1 Peter 2:23: "When he was reviled, he did not revile in return; when he suffered, he did not threaten, but continued entrusting himself to him who judges justly" (ESV). What a realization Peter must have had as he contemplated our Savior's response to the most justifiable situation for unforgiveness. But as we look at how Christ handled not just offense but legitimate physical and emotional harm, we can't help but yield to the Spirit as we work diligently to "send" offenses "away" and intentionally "grant" blessing to those who seemed to deserve it the least.

A last word here: forgiveness is also not the absence of consequences. God doesn't look the other way. As Galatians 6:7 teaches, you will reap what you sow. Moses suffered the consequences of his anger. David suffered the consequences of his actions toward Bathsheba and Uriah. Peter suffered the consequences of questioning the plan of God in the garden of Gethsemane. So there can be consequences for our actions (or the actions of those who harm us), but they aren't an excuse for us to not forgive.

In the remainder of this chapter, let's talk about what sending offenses away looks like in three scenarios: when pain is allowed by God, when pain is caused by others, and when pain is caused by self.

Pain Allowed by God

Let's get back to our two major ideas presented in Scripture. What we're really asking is how on earth we grant favor when we've been hurt, and how do we separate and "send away" the offenses that seem to come at us like daggers? And guess what? The major questions start with our relationship with God.

How many times has something happened in your life that made you wonder why God allowed it? You might think back on your childhood or teenage years to some pain, deep disappointment, or life-changing loss and wonder where God was in all of that. As an adult, a broken marriage, an unfavorable health diagnosis, or other crisis may have negatively marked you. Even if you are a follower of Christ and a true believer in the sovereignty of God—that He's ultimately in control—you could have experienced something that began to build a wall of resentment, distrust, or doubt.

What does all that mean? It means that before we can pursue forgiving others, we need to address any disconnect we have with God. Now, I would never say we need to "forgive" God. To say that would suggest God has a moral obligation or responsibility to His creation, which He does not. He is perfect and cannot morally fail. He doesn't need to be released of any offense. But despite the perfection of God, our hearts can still hold resentment toward Him. If not resentment, even a hint of doubt is damaging to our intimacy with the Father.

Throughout the Bible, we encounter many instances of God's people wrestling with feelings of disappointment, doubt, and despair. King David cried out, "Why, O Lord, do you stand far away? Why do you hide yourself in times of trouble?" (Ps. 10:1 ESV).

Feelings of disappointment or despair with God are not indicators of weak faith; rather, they are evidence of an engaged, authentic relationship with God. Like any relationship, our bond with God involves emotional peaks and valleys. Instead of trying to emotionally or psychologically "forgive" God, Scripture shows us that we can inquire of Him and He will answer. He will reveal His character to you, and what He shows you will invite you to worship, healing, and gratitude.

Your search may look like David's in Psalm 34:4.

> I sought the LORD and He answered me
> And rescued me from all my fears. (NASB)

Your seeking may look more like Job's, who reached the limit of his frustration, confusion, disillusionment, and so on, after being stripped of his family, possessions, status, and ultimately his health at the suggestion of God (Job 1:11–12; 2:3–6). After personal lament and receiving the advice of a few friends, Job finally questions God. In chapter 31, Job makes the case for his own character. Have you ever done that with God during a hard time? *Look, Lord, I've been upstanding, or at least I'm trying. How could this happen to a decent person like me?* Job is in that place. He is trying to make sense of what his life has become and in light of how he has lived with integrity for God. Then there's a little detour in the story as another friend (Elihu) speaks. But oh man, in chapter 38, God finally speaks. In chapters 38 and 39, God responds with an unmistakable reply. Instead of explaining Job's circumstances, or God's intentions, He proceeds to present the résumé of His character. Interestingly, His first words to Job are a question.

God asks,

> Will the faultfinder contend with the
>   Almighty?
> Let him who rebukes God give an answer.
>   (Job 40:2 NASB)

God is basically questioning how Job could question Him. It may seem cold and insensitive, but God knows exactly how to answer each of us. It seems that Job realizes immediately he may have gone too far (been there). Look at his response in verses 4 and 5.

> Behold, I am insignificant; what can I say in
>   response to You?
> I put my hand on my mouth.
> I have spoken once, and I will not reply;
> Or twice, and I will add nothing *more*.
>   (Job 40:4–5 NASB)

You know that moment when a child expresses themselves a little *too much* to a parent? I certainly had moments when the freedom to discuss my feelings and opinions with my dad needed to be reined in (And he gladly did it. Ha!) I imagine this moment happening with Job. A mental "uh-oh" if you will. But look at how God responds. He knows what we need to be reminded of. In this case He reminded Job of His omnipotence (absolute power). We read mind-blowing words like,

> Will you really nullify My judgment?
> Will you condemn Me so that you may be
>   justified? (Job 40:8 NASB)

Yet another reminder that while we may ask questions of God, regarding our lives and experiences, we do not question God's judgment. Like, ever. God continues through chapters 40 and 41 to show His power in creation. Because Job truly had a heart for God, he was able to respond to God's reply with worship because he understands God's response is just. It gave him divine clarity. One of my favorite verses in Scripture is found in Job's confession following God's revelation of His character. In Job 42:5–6 (NASB), he reveals,

> I have heard of You by the hearing of the ear;
> But now my eye sees You;
> Therefore I retract,
> And I repent, sitting on dust and ashes.

Do you see that powerful revelation? Job is basically realizing that despite all of the pain he's experienced, it pales in comparison to the character and work of God. This realization is so jarring that Job admits his knowledge of God has shifted from a type of blind awareness to a more meaningful comprehension. Now his eyes are opened to the power, goodness, and justice of God (even when his life felt unfair). This realization makes way for repentance and worship. David had a similar response if you look back at Psalm 34:8 (NASB). David exclaims,

Taste and see that the LORD is good;
How blessed is the man who takes refuge in
Him!

David's exclamation about the Lord's goodness was not because his circumstances had changed. He wrote Psalm 34 when his life was under such serious threat from Saul that David pretended to be insane to avoid capture. (Read 1 Samuel 21.) These were hard times, y'all. But still David sought the Lord and was rescued. *Not rescued from his enemies, but rescued from his fears.* This is how it works. Whatever your fear, whatever your hurt or wound, God can and *will* rescue you, and He'll do it in the exact way you need it for His glory and your healing.

Going back to Job's response, you may be wondering how on earth your trauma or pain will lead to *your* repentance. Only when you authentically seek to know God and share your pain with Him will you land in a place of deeper worship. Remember, *asking God questions isn't the same thing as questioning God.* Job certainly didn't hold back his anger and frustrations with God, but he shared it *with* God and not *about* God to others. In Job 42:7–9 God clearly states that His anger burned against Job's friends and not against Job himself. Why? Because of how they spoke of Him. *God didn't count Job's discourse as dishonor.* He still favored him and restored him beyond his original station.

Friend, share your hurt with the Father. Share it authentically. I know I have told God many feelings and frustrations with raw emotions. God is not offended by authenticity.

Inquire of Him. Seek Him and see what His Word has to say. Acknowledge your feelings of anger or betrayal, process those emotions, then release them and allow yourself to trust in God's goodness and sovereignty once again. Let the freedom of Proverbs 3:5–6 sink in: "Trust in the LORD with all your heart, and do not lean on your own understanding. In all your ways acknowledge him, and he will make straight your paths" (ESV). Come to terms with who He is and His immeasurable goodness that has never left you. Don't expect it to happen overnight. It might. But it might not.

If you're wrestling with these feelings, you're not alone. Disillusionment with God is a shared human experience and requires a compassionate, introspective, and grace-filled response. Confessing these feelings to God builds intimacy with Him and tears down the protective walls that pain builds. It's ultimately about adjusting our perspective through an understanding that both God's wisdom *and* love transcend our human comprehension. This is the reason we can agree with Isaiah 55:8–9 when he writes, "For my thoughts are not your thoughts, neither are your ways my ways, declares the LORD. For as the heavens are higher than the earth, so are my ways higher than your ways and my thoughts than your thoughts" (ESV). And we can resonate with Paul's conclusion in Romans 8:38–39: "For I am sure that neither death nor life, nor angels nor rulers, nor things present nor things to come, nor powers, nor height nor depth, nor anything else in all creation, will be able to separate us from the love of God in Christ Jesus our Lord" (ESV).

Now that we have laid a path for dealing with pain allowed by God, we can begin to address the pain caused by people. Just like the command to love, it always starts with how we connect with God before we can look at how we connect to people. The truth is, our dysfunctional and unhealthy relationship traits come from dysfunctional and unhealthy beliefs about God. If you get serious about being close to God and knowing Him, you will pave the way for real intimacy with others (which requires constant forgiveness). Unforgiveness, in any form, to any degree, works in opposition to love.

Do you see why divine love must always be forgiving? Do you understand why we must work to release pain, send away offenses, and divorce ourselves from despair? Is it clear why forgiving doesn't end with releasing but with bestowing and blessing? That's a lot to digest. Feel free to pause here and just write down some thoughts.

Pain Caused by Others

As the ideas around forgiveness stir in your mind and spirit, you will probably start to wonder how this impacts your relationships with people who have hurt you. We all have stories and experiences around being hurt by others. Sometimes it's a close friend or family member; other times it's a spouse. There are even times when someone we don't know very well somehow hurts us deeply. God knew this kind of pain would be a part of the human experience, and He tells us exactly what to do with it in Colossians 3:12–14 (ESV):

> Put on then, as God's chosen ones, holy and
> beloved, compassionate hearts, kindness,
> humility, meekness, and patience, bearing
> with one another and, if one has a complaint
> against another, **forgiving each other**; as
> the Lord has forgiven you, so you also must
> forgive. And above all these put on **love**,
> which binds everything together in perfect
> harmony.

In Paul's instruction, we see forgiveness as a part of a much broader context. We are called to holiness, compassion, kindness, and so on. But it can't be separated from a spirit of forgiveness, and forgiveness can't be separated from love. Do you want to guess what word here is translated "love"? You got it. *Agape.* That is the kind of love that allows us to forgive others. *Agape* is so comprehensive that forgiving others is just one of many choices we make when we pursue the highest calling of love. We can't separate forgiveness from all the other things God calls us to do and be.

The bottom line is that *forgiveness is necessary for fullness* in your spiritual life. So, how can we practically begin to carry a spirit of forgiveness into all our relationships? We need to embrace the truth that while forgiveness won't be convenient or comfortable, it is not optional. Forgiveness does not require anyone else to be involved; I can resolve that between myself and God. Before we get that apology or that explanation, we can still find closure because that is a gift from God.

I have found that I need to approach forgiveness from two angles. The first way is *specific forgiveness* and the second way is the *cycle of forgiveness*. These are terms I have coined to describe the two major pathways of forgiveness we all need to be on.

1. Specific forgiveness draws us in to focus on specific traumatic or extremely hurtful situations we have experienced that marked us significantly. That experience could range from some form of abuse to a deep betrayal by a friend or spouse. When we are dealing with specific incidents of offense or betrayal, we need a targeted approach to forgiveness. That means inviting God into a specific pain and seeking His guidance on how you send it away or release it and eventually become able to offer favor. This might require counseling or professional help or may be resolved in your personal communion with Jesus and your healthy community with friends. Depending on the level of pain or offense, specific forgiveness can take time as layers of hurt and subsequent coping mechanisms are pulled back. Even if the person you are forgiving is no longer alive or is someone you may never see or speak to again, there is so much value in releasing the pain, betrayal, rejection, abandonment, and so on. Only God Himself can help you do that. (Also, if you are processing any type of abuse, I repeat again that you should seek additional help. Forgiveness does not mean "letting the abuser off the hook." Your job is to do the spiritual work, but if someone has physically harmed you or broken the law, it is the state's job to do the legal work.)

2. The cycle of forgiveness is the ongoing practice of seeking to release, send away, or divorce oneself from offense.

This aspect of forgiveness moves past a specific pain and begins to change how we handle future offenses. But that must happen in layers or cycles. Think about a clock. Not a digital display but an analog clock with a short hand and a long hand (and typically a second hand). If you think about how that clock moves, you'll realize that multiple cycles are happening to create accuracy. The second hand travels around the clock every sixty seconds. The minute hand is traveling around the clock every sixty minutes. And then the hour hand is traveling around the clock every twelve hours. This rhythm reminds me of the cycle of forgiveness (figuratively speaking of course).

There are going to be sixty-second releases because the offense was minor. Someone was rude and cut you off in traffic, or a personal joke was made at your expense. Maybe someone didn't text you back or invite you to something you wanted to attend. Maybe you have to deal with the person who does not share your expectations, and that disconnect shows up in whatever relationship you have with this person. For example, a spouse that doesn't share your standard of cleanliness or a colleague who doesn't share your work ethic.

There are going to be sixty-minute releases. This may involve something that hurts a little deeper than the previously mentioned offenses. Maybe a friend really did betray your trust. Or there could have been hurtful words that you received from someone who knows how to hurt you because you've been vulnerable with them. Maybe in your career a superior or a peer was clearly trying to negatively impact your work and success.

Then there are going to be some **twelve- or twenty-four-hour releases.** These are our midterm forgiveness projects. When I say midterm, I don't mean how long it takes to forgive (because that can happen instantly when you choose to trust Jesus in the darkest places, or other times it may take more time). The midterm aspect of this comes with the healing portion. I can release the debt and decide that the other person does not owe me. Like my four-year-old self quickly released the hurt created by my preteen next-door neighbor for thinking that putting me on a ten-speed bike was a good idea in the first place. But the actual healing of the wound took much longer (and that was a physical wound).

Of course, these "cycles" look different in each of our lives. Things that might be a sixty-second release for one person may be a twelve-hour release process for another person. It will vary depending on our preexisting pain and triggers, but we need to commit to regular evaluations of what we need to release. That's actually the point of Communion. A rhythm of reflection. Jesus asks us to remember His death through confession and forgiveness as often as possible.

Let's go a step further—the ultimate goal is the ability to bestow blessing or favor on those who have offended or hurt us, as we read about in Romans 12 earlier. We seek to bless and not curse others, even our enemies. We seek to repay evil with good.

What do I mean by blessings or favor toward a neighbor who hurt us? I don't mean gifts or tangible things, but the ability to pray for those who have caused significant pain for us is a sign of true forgiveness and the model that was given by Jesus in His most vulnerable hour as noted in Luke 23:34: "Father, forgive them, for they know not what they do" (ESV).

This may seem like an unattainable goal. It may feel completely unrealistic, but don't focus on that. Focus on the *rhythm* or the *approach*. And the rhythm is bigger than just a means to an end. You're not just trying to achieve some false sense of "being okay" because you're able to forgive others quickly. The goal is to grow in self-awareness, knowledge of God, awareness and knowledge of others, with a yieldedness to the Holy Spirit so that we might see the offense differently in the beginning.

And for the record, I don't want to just develop a habit of being hurt and trying to let it go. **I want to also do the work to figure out why certain things offend me in the first place.** When I look at Jesus's powerful request for forgiveness as He hung on a cross He did not deserve, I am acutely aware that the Lord has equipped me to do the same. Do you know why Jesus was able to make such a counter-intuitive request? It certainly wasn't hinging on the thieves offering apology or explanation for their actions. It hinged on a Savior who was fully aware, fully confident, and fully committed to His mission even in the midst of vulnerability. As you think about your cycles for forgiveness, ask yourself where you feel unsteady or insecure. Those will be the places that will create the biggest challenge for you receiving and offering forgiveness. In our areas of vulnerability, we tend to have blurred vision, which means we are more easily offended, more deeply hurt, so we need heightened awareness if we're going to change course.

Whether you're dealing with a need for *specific* forgiveness or working on the cycle of forgiveness, know that God is able to meet you in either place and in both places at the same time. These are not parallel paths. Forgiveness calls out the weakness, pride, and pain in our humanity. To do it God's way, we need God's guidance.

It will be tempting, but let me challenge you not to push the issue aside. Don't put it in the closet or stuff it under the bed. Invite God in because the reality is it's spiritually, emotionally, and physically impossible to love well without also having an intentional pursuit of forgiveness. Do you see how this is a whole new way to love your neighbor? When the people of the world see this, or experience it from you directly, they marvel. They wonder where you could have found that kind of power, and they will be full of questions about the validity of your freedom. And when their questions come, wondering where you found the ability to be this free, you'll be able to share the answer: Jesus.

Pain Caused by Self

One last thing. What about the need to forgive ourselves? Do you need to forgive *you*? The pain we inflict on ourselves can easily go unnoticed. We talk down to ourselves when we fail, we blame ourselves for pain that others caused. Sometimes we hold ourselves in the light of someone else's life, and we berate ourselves for not being *good enough*.

Then there is guilt and shame. The guilt starts as soon as we make a decision (no matter how small) that collides with our conscience. Soon after, guilt brings a "plus one" to the party, and shame is the partner of choice. We carry shame for so many reasons and at varying depths for the mistakes we've authored and for some we haven't. Essentially, guilt is the horrible feeling after doing something wrong (directly or indirectly), and shame is the horrible worry that it will be exposed. Those thoughts of self-loathing can affect every aspect of our health, the way we relate to God and to people.

If this is where you are today, I highly recommend Curt Thompson's *The Soul of Shame* as a resource. We have to work to change the narrative in our minds. We can be convicted by our decisions and still give ourselves grace. We can learn from mistakes and swim in God's mercy. We can learn to be better without beating ourselves up. We can rehearse the truth of the gospel to ourselves: *we've been forgiven our debts*. Every single one of them. Past, present, and future.

At the heart of healing from the self-inflicted pain is what we believe about God. It is the foundation for everything. It's the reason I spent the majority of this chapter addressing our disconnect with God. As you dig into the offending self-talk that you need to "send away," you will face what you think about God. Why? Because it's all connected. We are made in His image (Gen. 1:26), which means we are created to resemble Him. Remember, He forgave first. He set the example. Forgiving ourselves and others is one clear way to be like Him.

When we have a false understanding of ourselves, it is evidence of a false understanding of God. The only way to begin to address that is to go back to the beginning. Ask your Creator to remind you of His idea of you and to redirect you toward a path of healing and restoration—not just for your own satisfaction but so you can love the way He expects you to.

Prayer: *Lord, You know my life and You know my pain. You know all the offenses I need to release, and You see how forgiveness is a thief of true freedom. Lord, please prepare my heart to begin this journey of forgiveness. I know it won't be easy, but it is necessary, and with You it's possible. Remind me of the forgiveness I have received from You, and show me how to release others and seek healing for myself. In a world that holds grudges, help me love in this new way. Amen.*

Chapter 7

BE BRAVE: Love Is Uncomfortable

'm listening to my kids argue over who's touching whom as they watch a movie lying next to each other on the couch. All I hear is "Move your foot!" "Chloe, stop!" "Joah, move!" They insisted on watching a movie and have been looking forward to it all day. Generally, they get along (as much as a seven-year-old girl and an eleven-year-old boy can). They play, laugh, and argue. They defend each other and protect each other. Their sibling love is beautiful to watch. Most of the time, they have total freedom with each other. They wrestle, build, create, and compete in intense soccer matches and dance competitions. They engage in a fluid and organic way with the occasional altercation. (And by occasional, I mean several times a day.) They bounce back quickly and move on to reengagement.

But every now and then, the disagreement lasts for a little while. When that happens, everything is an issue. One is "too close" to the other. One is "looking" at the other. You know, basically, all the things that don't bother them when they are at peace. In short, even though they love each other, they have moments when they set boundaries with each other.

One afternoon, I heard them arguing and setting these sorts of boundaries, and I remember going to the pantry to get something and coming back to an entirely different scene. Chloe had hit her knee on the coffee table, and Joah was tending to her. She was crying, and he was "big-brothering." It was a remarkable sight. Yes, it was tender and sweet, but it was also night and day. I tried to process what I was seeing compared to what I know transpired just moments earlier. It started to make a little sense. As I watched them, I witnessed how easily their love rose above the moment. *Even in the middle of their disagreement, that love never left.* That is why, at the right time, they were able to reconnect and reestablish their relationship. *I was able to see a glimpse of what is possible for us as adults.*

Most of us have experienced layers of pain and complex disappointments, and even though we have moments we need to draw boundaries with others, *unconditional love is possible.* Even through the discomfort.

Many times life demands we set boundaries in our relationships and create space from unhealthy circumstances. But love is so much bigger and braver than boundaries. God demonstrated it and calls us to the same transcendent love. It's possible to have guidelines that govern a relationship without lessening our love. **Boundaries don't negate love, and distance doesn't have to mean disconnection. There is**

a way to set healthy boundaries that still give us the space to love the people we need distance from.

How do we do that? How do we set boundaries that are built on God's wisdom rather than our wound? How do we love through the discomfort? The answer is in the Scriptures.

Godly Boundaries in Scripture

I'll start with this: God knows that *agape* (love) doesn't mean equal access to all. Boundaries do have a place in loving relationships.

First, at the basic level of boundary setting, we have a foundational truth found in Proverbs 4:23: "Above all else, guard your heart, for everything you do flows from it" (NIV). This verse emphasizes the importance of protecting and setting boundaries for one's heart, which as we discussed in chapter 2, encompasses emotions, thoughts, and desires.

This proverb is found in the midst of many pieces of wisdom a father is giving his son. It's not specific to a certain type of relationship, and it doesn't detail exactly *what* we need to be guarding our hearts from. But its presence in Scripture makes a powerful statement, and that is this: **We are expected to decide who has access to our hearts.**

It also means we are *continuously* guarding our hearts. Who has access today may not be the same people who have access next year. The opposite is also true. Over time, the person we need distance from today may evolve while we also mature. As a result, we may not need the same distance from them in six months.

We must invite God's wisdom to know *whom* to bring close and *how close* to bring them. We are careful with our hearts because it's the essence of who we are, and according to the verse, everything we do flows from it.

> **We are expected to decide who has access to our hearts.**

My husband and I use this passage often as we are counseling couples who are dating, but it applies to every relationship. Sometimes we need to protect our hearts from family members, friends, or spouses. If we are pursuing *agape* with all of who we are, we will ask God for the best way to do it. And here's the promise. God will show us how do it in a way that honors Him and frees us to love well, even if that love is at a distance. Only God can show you how to guard your heart without self-protection since He gives you the guidance, He is still the protector. He doesn't want you to create your own boundaries, but, instead, apply the boundaries He sets for you.

A second passage speaks to how we should set boundaries with worldliness and worldly people. Psalm 1:1 (NIV) says,

> Blessed is the one
>> who does not walk in step with the wicked
> or stand in the way that sinners take
>> or sit in the company of mockers.

This wisdom is more specific than Proverbs 4:23 because it specifies how we interact with certain people. We can't align ourselves with those not aligned with God, and we can't walk in the same ways as those not seeking to imitate Christ. This doesn't mean we avoid building relationships with non-Christians. In fact, Scripture calls us to draw near to sinners just as Christ did. The boundary here means we don't "walk in step" with the wisdom unbelievers live by. We can love a person without subscribing to any belief or practice that goes against God's standards.

Here's one more verse to consider when it comes to the power of boundaries. Proverbs 25:28 says, "Like a city whose walls are broken through is a person who lacks self-control" (NIV).

Now, this passage speaks directly to our own self-control as a wise boundary of protection. Basically, there will be times when you need to set boundaries with a person because you lack the self-control to not get angry all over again or be rude or distant. If someone has hurt you but you're not ready to spend time with them, you might need space for a season while you do the work of forgiveness and healing. Or there may be a friend you have an unhealthy attraction toward. Set a boundary. Married or single, we can't love people well if our emotions cloud our judgment. We need boundaries as we grow in self-control. You may have an ex who brings out the worst in you; that's a prime opportunity to set a wise boundary.

There are other examples we could easily observe in Scripture when it comes to godly boundaries: In Genesis 2:16, Adam and Eve were told there was one tree they could *not* eat from (the tree of knowing about not just good but also evil). Distance from evil is a good thing. In Exodus 23:32, God tells us not to worship other gods—that's a boundary. Distance from false gods is a good thing.

I could go on, but the overall point is this: godly, biblical boundaries create distance in the places we truly need it, and it's right to follow these boundaries because *God* is the one who placed them there for our good.

But what about the kind of boundaries God never set? What do we do with the commonly accepted "boundaries" our culture tells us to draw? What about the ones that come not from God's Word but the world?

Worldly Boundaries

Our culture is big on drawing lines and setting limitations with attached ultimatums. There is a deep inclination (sometimes premature) toward boundaries. We say, "If you cross this line, I'm leaving," without seeking to understand intentions or initiating to repair the relationship. We decide what "too far" is and quickly hand out consequences while withholding grace. Don't get me wrong; there are certainly times when boundaries and distance are needed for emotional and/or physical safety. In other instances, boundaries are needed because God is disciplining someone, and He wants to make sure we are out of the way. But too often, boundaries are expressions of the values of our culture, and they are driven by self-protection rather than God-led wisdom. Said another way, we create distance with worldly boundaries sometimes because we're afraid of getting hurt.

Here's what that can look like:

- Someone betrays your trust, and you swiftly sever the relationship because dishonesty is the "one thing" you can't tolerate. You have forgotten how many times you have been dishonest with God, and/or you're unwilling to have a hard conversation to strengthen a friendship or demonstrate inconvenient, sacrificial love.

- A coworker continues to demonstrate an inability to complete the task to your standard, so you permanently exclude him or her from advancement opportunities. You're deciding they can't change or you're unwilling to help.

- Your spouse says or does that thing that gets under your skin, so you become emotionally unavailable until some unknown time in the future to teach a "lesson."

- You have a friend who has not been as intentional in his or her spiritual journey, and now your interests and values have drifted. You decide to remove the friendship completely from your life rather than navigate a new way to love.

In all these examples and more, we see that the world's way of establishing boundaries has conditioned us toward either creating *distance* or simply *dismantling* the whole relationship when we feel hurt, betrayed, or frustrated. Where God wants reconciliation in our everyday relationships, the world uses a "boundary" to divide them, and the underlying issue is one of trust. If you don't trust God to protect you, you will make it your business to protect yourself.

Healing the Divide

Agape offers us a new way to handle these everyday relational divides, and as always, it uses God as our example. One look at 2 Corinthians 5:19 (NASB1995) will show us this. It reminds us of two important truths: (1) We were all running away from Christ. And (2) Christ made the first move *toward* us instead of away from us. It reads:

> God was in Christ reconciling the world to Himself, not counting their trespasses against them, and He has committed to us the word of reconciliation.

Christ was bringing us to Himself. He has always been looking to reestablish the connection with Him that we broke due to sin. Consider Romans 5:8 (NASB1995) for more proof. It tells us:

> But God demonstrates His own love toward us, in that while we were yet sinners, Christ died for us.

Let that sink in. While we were betraying God with our own ignorance, arrogance, self-promotion, and self-protection—when we were at our worst—He didn't draw a boundary with us. He didn't decide to steer clear of our toxic and rebellious posture toward Him. He didn't cut us off or shut us out. He created a way to bring us close. When we did everything to create a wider gap between Himself and us, He *closed* it. And He didn't change who He was. He didn't lower the standard. The standard of required righteousness remained, but He sent His Son to help us meet the standard. What Jesus did for you, He can also do *through* you as you love others.

If you feel overwhelmed, you're getting the point. This should feel overwhelming. God loves us with an initiating love. He loved us first and continues to love us first. *At every breech in our relationship with Him, He extends His love; therefore, at every breech in our human relationships, we must do the same.* Said another way, when there is a rift in a relationship, our culture says to run as fast as you can. To simply give up. To call any level of relational difficulty "toxic" and just be done with the whole thing. But *agape* is different. It's a whole new way to love and handle boundaries. Divine love gets uncomfortable and makes the first move to reestablish the connection.

Before you get scared and start thinking of all the exceptions to this, or all the ways you could be exposing yourself to hurt, remember that **love without condition doesn't equate to love without wisdom.** There is space to continuously and sacrificially love a person you don't have physical or emotional proximity to.

What Would This Look Like?

Think about this scenario. Let's say you are betrayed by a friend. This friend breaks your confidence and shares something personal you entrusted to them. What do you do? Do you cut them off? Do you set a boundary that keeps them at arm's length with no explanation? Do you pretend you've dealt with it but harbor bitterness? If you are inviting God into that pain and asking Him how to love with an initiating love, you might find yourself in a countercultural scenario. The Holy Spirit might remind you of a few important things.

He may whisper a reminder that you are to love others as Christ has loved you (John 13:34). Or He may recount to you the ways you have betrayed Christ's trust or proven undeserving of His love (Rom. 3:23). The Spirit of God may point you to tell the truth in love (Eph. 4:15). He may remind you to humbly control yourself, lovingly confront sin, graciously accept others, and overcome evil with good (Rom. 12:21). Or He may remind you that God promises wisdom in every circumstance (James 1:5). In all these ways and more, the Spirit of God who lives inside you will help you love like God loves—with a love that goes first and moves *toward* the other person to repair the rift.

> Love without condition does not equate to love without wisdom.

If you're wondering if this is really possible, remember the life of Peter (his story is in the Gospels). He was one of Jesus's chief disciples and dearest friends, but he denied Jesus three times out of fear. Peter was too afraid to be associated with Jesus when he thought it might be risky. But ultimately, he was the poster child of grace and undeserving love. Jesus moved toward Peter, even at his worst, and restored Peter by giving him a chance to declare his love for his Savior rather than deny it. Jesus loved Peter enough to know what was coming (Matt. 26:34), invite him into his most vulnerable space (Matt. 26:36–37), and have a plan for not only restoration but a leadership position that would alter history (John 21:15–19). He loves you like that, too. And He can love *through* you like that in your relationship with others. It may feel scary or risky, but through the power of God's Spirit you are brave enough to go first and move toward someone who has offended you, it really is possible. Where the world runs away in fear of a broken relationship, *agape* (love) is brave. It makes the first move.

Taking the Lead

As you let your heart and mind settle—or wrestle—with this new and divine way of loving, you may have feelings of gratitude and frustration. You'll be grateful for the unreasonable way Christ loves you, and you'll likely feel frustrated (or slightly defeated) with what you know He requires of you. I know the conflicting truths that sit in my own soul. I am by nature tempted to respond to pain or offense in ways that prioritize me and my comfort. I know my tendency to be defensive or distant in the name of boundaries without having ever asked God what I should do. When I ask God what I should do (and actually take the time to listen and respond accordingly), I find myself in unexplainable situations. I find myself initiating love even if it's unseen by others.

I've dealt with betrayal from a friend, and everything in me wants to lash out. You may be the opposite and lean toward shutting down. However we respond, there's a tendency to want to make my case and/or withhold my love, which then makes the relationship a debt–debtor relationship. If I decide to stay in the friendship, something in me wants that person to know they "owe me" for staying. But this is a worldly way of thinking; a godly way to handle it would be to offer love in the way that God guides me without broadcasting it. Trying to love like Christ means considering what this person actually needs and understanding the scenario with as much objectivity and wisdom as possible. It also means deciding whether this merits a conversation or feedback, and if it does, when does that happen, how does that happen, and who takes the lead on making that happen?

I know this may seem like a lot of thinking and processing, but in the work of love, it's what we're called to do. Here's the good news: the more you do it, the faster you'll be able to do it. You can come to a point to be able to objectively assess a scenario and make a God-honoring decision. *God-honoring decisions* mean we are not giving in to the plans of the enemy, and we trust He will give us a supernatural capacity to look like—and respond like—our Savior. In the midst of pain and offense, we are able to say, "Father, forgive them, for they know not what they do." This is what it means to make the first move. It's a heart posture before it's an outward gesture.

We are able to pray for the one who hurt us and be genuinely concerned about their heart and their relationship with God. We are able to sincerely ask for God's blessing and favor over their lives. The blessing might be for their salvation or spiritual healing. And even for those with evil intentions, if God asks us to break bread with them, we can do it the way Jesus did with Judas. The words of Romans 8 will ring true, "If our God is for us who can be against us" (v. 31 ESV).

It really is amazing when divine love reveals itself to you and moves through you. Even as we deal with deeper pain such as abuse and harm in our past, through the strength of the Holy Spirit (and usually at a distance from the other person), we can get to a place where we love the offender as much as God does, and we can have a heart like our Savior's that prioritizes the redemption of souls and the rebuilding of lives. Because we have God's Spirit moving through us in love toward others, we can rest in His strength and trust God with the results of the other person.

Just think about our Savior's ability to separate His personal feelings of agony and pain while on the cross from the ultimate goal of reconciling us to God. It was possible for Him to feel the pain and still make the sacrifice for our good. He could do both. *Agape* does both. And so can we. It's as if Jesus is whispering, "If I can love Judas and invite him to the final supper and wash his feet, out of obedience, surely you can love the one who's hurt you." And by *love*, remember, we don't mean "just act like nothing happened." We mean to bestow favor or to bless. Real healing is evident when we can do this. As discussed in chapter 6 of this book, this is almost unheard of. Forgiving is one thing, but the bravery required to request blessing on their behalf is another story altogether. It's unlike anything our world can wrap its head around. It's a whole new way to love.

When It's Complicated, Wisdom and Willingness

You may be asking at this point, "But what about those relationships where it's really complicated?"

- The friend who keeps breaking your trust
- The adult who traumatized you as a child
- The spouse who betrayed you
- The person who deceived you

The scenarios of pain are so similar and yet different. We all have multiple stories of betrayal and hurt. But how do we reconcile the legitimate hurt caused by others and the command to love? I believe it requires *divine wisdom* and *divine willingness.*

Divine wisdom is the Holy Spirit's way of applying truth to guide our decision-making. In the above examples, it means following God's guidance on setting healthy boundaries and creating necessary space. *He will show you how to be discerning about someone's weakness without holding it against them.* The discernment God gives is to accomplish His purpose. His aim is that we love Him with all we are and love people the way He loves us. God's divine wisdom is found in four primary places: His Word, His Son, His Spirit, and His people. Said another way, look to Scripture, the example of Christ, the power of the Holy Spirit, and the counsel of godly people to help you make decisions on how to love another person when the situation is complicated.

For example, God's Spirit may show you a path to healing from past trauma, but that path will not shut down the capacity to love. The wisdom He gives shouldn't cancel out our willingness to love. In another example, let's say you have a friend who always wants to hang out but never wants to go deep (I have one of these). God may reveal that this friend's tendency doesn't give you the right to minimize time with her (as He revealed to me). We may be tempted to try "nice avoidance," but God may reveal that your friend is afraid of rejection. He may give you guidance, as He did with me, on how to deepen your vulnerability and help you authentically reengage. When it comes to my own situation with a friend, I'm so glad I made the first move. God worked in our friendship, and it's been richer than I could have imagined.

Why did I reengage? Because on the coin of loving well, *the flip side of divine wisdom is divine willingness.* God is responsible for the wisdom; He must give that to us and empower us. Our side of the equation is to be willing to go first. To initiate. To move toward a rift, not away. In short, we must choose to be brave. To trust that God will give us the wisdom and take the first step toward the other person. I call it "divine" willingness because even our courage is empowered by God Himself. With His Spirit inside of us, we have all the power we need to be brave and take the lead.

How about a marriage example? Let's say your marriage has been coasting along for fourteen years and suddenly hits a rough spot. It isn't recognizable because careers and family seem to be thriving, but intimacy is declining. You have a list of reasons for the decline, and 90 percent of them are your spouse's fault. You complain to the Lord, give Him your evidence, and make your case. If you keep your heart and mind open to the voice of the Lord, and you ask Him for divine wisdom, He will speak. It may be through His Word, through the example of His Son Jesus, through His people's counsel, or perhaps through that still small voice of His Spirit inside. Regardless of how, it will probably happen at the most unexpected time. Right when you expect the Lord to come to your defense, He calls you to a divine love that opens your eyes to your own weaknesses, moves toward your spouse, and sincerely takes your part of the blame. And all the while, God shows you that your spouse's weaknesses, though real and sometimes hurtful, are not a tool for shame but rather something to steward, pray for, and communicate constructively about. In one moment, right in the middle of the discomfort, the Lord shows you opportunities for *agape*.

Divine wisdom and divine willingness bring divine revelation. God is faithful to show us a new approach to loving well. It doesn't mean we ignore conflict. It means we address it from a place of security and understanding. By the way, understanding doesn't mean agreement. You can choose to "see" someone and acknowledge who they are and where they are without agreeing. The point is not to agree on everything under the sun; the point is *restored relationship*. Remember, the world has trained us to create distance anytime we feel anything negative in a relationship. But God's love (*agape*) shows us a new and better way—an approach that reestablishes the relational bond by moving toward the other person instead of away. This kind of love is okay with the situation feeling uncomfortable; it can move through that discomfort with bravery. Why? Because, for one, the state of the relationship matters more than the comfort level. And two, this is the way God loved us and how He expects us to love others.

Prayer: *God, please show me how to be brave and go first in the relational rifts I have. Help me move toward my offender in the way You moved toward me in the gospel. Keep me from running to self-protection, and remind me that You are my ultimate protector. As for the relationships that do require a safe distance, help me set boundaries that still honor You. I want to guard my heart and remain available to love (agape) the way you call me to. You are the only wise God, and only You can show me how to love well the people You put in my life. Help me to be honest with myself so my boundaries aren't ties to unforgiveness. Give me divine willingness and divine wisdom, and help me seek the best in others so I know when to change a boundary and bring them closer. Most of all, help me be the kind of person who is safe for others so Your name may be glorified. In Jesus's name, amen.*

Chapter 8

BE RESILIENT: Love Is Unrelenting

One of my close friends has had a lifelong, tumultuous relationship with her mother. I don't mean daily arguments or constant disagreements. I'm talking about deep offenses and betrayals that would lead to months or years of no communication. Her mother has a terrible pattern of trying to control people's lives, and if you don't comply, you'll be cut off. She can cut you down without a second thought.

For the last forty years my friend has lived in constant disappointment. She and her mother will have good days, weeks, or even months, and then something happens. Some family gossip will prove to be true, and she'll find out that, once again, her mother has chosen self-interest over her daughter.

As her friend, my heart breaks every time I hear of yet another fracture in their relationship. But I have to challenge my friend that although her mother's actions don't invite praise, don't exempt her from love. Not mechanical, obligatory love but *agape*.

Telling a hurting friend (especially a hurting daughter) to still love her mother is not an easy conversation, no matter how much she loves Jesus. I have helped her seek God on biblical boundaries and encouraged her to resist the resentment that constantly threatens to set in. I gently remind her that love doesn't give up. It is unrelenting.

Why would I encourage her in this way? Because God's love didn't give up on her (or me). So it must be possible to persevere in her pursuit of divine love (*agape*) as well. God expects it from her (and us) in her relationships with others—toxic, dysfunctional mother included.

I'm not sure if you've been in this type of situation or something similar, but this is where our beliefs are tested. This where we have to decide if the new way to love our neighbor is great material for knowledge or great material for *life*.

Unrelenting, Resilient, and Hopeful Love

We've been talking about a new kind of love in this book—God's *agape* (love). We've talked about how this kind of love is curious (always learning) and free (always forgiving). And in the chapter before this one, we talked about love being brave, requiring us to be uncomfortable. So, how is resilient, unrelenting love different? Here's the difference: resilience requires us to be uncomfortable and initiate even when someone hurts us, but being relentless takes it a step further. It does everything we've talked about *but over and over again*, even when relationships continue to be challenging. We are called to express love in all the ways we've talked about so far but not just once or twice—for a lifetime. The apostle Paul knew how hard this would be when he encouraged us to "not become weary in doing good" in Galatians 6:9. We are challenged to stay the course and be relentless in our efforts to love like Christ.

But where could we get the kind of power to keep going even when those we love continue to be difficult? How do we keep from quitting?

Consider this: loving others in an unrelenting way requires two important things. The first is *confidence* and the second is *patience*. Where did I get this? Hebrews 11:1 says, "Now faith is the **assurance** of things **hoped** for, the conviction of things not seen" (ESV).

The rest of that chapter goes on to detail many "heroes" of our faith and what they did that was noteworthy. But the key words are *assurance* and *hoped*. The word *assurance* speaks to confidence or certainty. The word *hoped* speaks to a divine patience. It is a grounded anticipation, and it definitely requires patience—which is another way of saying fortitude, perseverance, endurance, or an unrelenting will to keep going. It's that thing in a person that just keeps at it no matter what. It's the ability to bounce back even after something hard happens. It is a

Belief in the *unseen* does not mean belief in the *unknown*.

reminder that faith, or belief in the *unseen*, does not mean belief in the *unknown*.

You may be wondering why I used a verse about faith to talk about love. When we contemplate the love God calls us to exhibit, don't we conclude that it requires faith? How can we, as finite, flawed human beings, even believe we can love the way God requires? It demands faith. Faith is more than the belief of what God can and will do. It is equally the belief of what we can do *with God*. Not knowing something and not seeing something are two vastly different realities.

I can not see my friend for months and years due to various reasons, but I still have every assurance that she's there and she's my friend. I may not *see* her, but there is no question that I *know* her. In this case, if I needed something from her or needed to call for guidance or for nothing at all, I know that when we connect it will be meaningful and filling. So I don't need to have faith to know whether our connection will be impactful.

On the other hand, if there's someone to whom I've just been introduced and I work with her regularly but have never had longer than a three-minute conversation with her, I would have feelings of doubt if I needed to depend on her as a friend. I see her often but I don't *know* her. This distinction is important because *when we talk about the unrelenting nature of God's love, and the love to which He's called us, we are not talking about an ignorant or uninformed love but a love that has proven itself time after time.*

Consider 1 Corinthians 13:7. It speaks to a love that "hopes all things." What does that mean? It's talking about an intelligent love, one that's knowledgeable of its source and aware of potential failures but is so anchored in God that it cannot help but exhibit hope or divine certainty. It's the hope David displayed in Psalm 40 when he says he waited patiently for the Lord and the Lord answered him and inclined Himself toward David. *His waiting was not the same as wondering.* He had confidence that the Lord would respond, and so his waiting was anchored and confident. *David's assurance anchored his patience, and ours must do the same.* That is the divine hope that God calls us to as we love well.

When we do this, we are not riddled with doubt and insecurity. We can have hope for ourselves because we know the character of the God we love and serve. He's the God who keeps His promises. More than that, we can have *intercessory hope*, as I like to call it. That is holding out hope on behalf of another. We don't have to be overcome with despair, anxiety, or fear of the unknown because what we need to know, we do in fact know. And that is the character and nature of God. So we can face the *unseen* because we are anchored in the *known*.

Understanding the necessity for confidence and patience and believing God is the source of both gives us the divine capacity to love with hope. It allows us to continue to love people when their actions don't earn it. It's a new way to love in a world overcome by doubt, cynicism, and abandonment when it gets too uncomfortable.

An Example

Do you want to read about one of the most uncomfortable situations in life? Check out what Jesus's father, Joseph, had to process in Matthew 1:18–21 (ESV):

> Now the birth of Jesus Christ took place in this way. When his mother Mary had been betrothed to Joseph, before they came together she was found to be with child from the Holy Spirit. And her husband Joseph, being a just man and unwilling to put her to shame, resolved to divorce her quietly. But as he considered these things, behold, an angel of the Lord appeared to him in a dream, saying, "Joseph, son of David, do not fear to take Mary as your wife, for that which is conceived in her is from the Holy Spirit. She will bear a son, and you shall call his name Jesus, for he will save his people from their sins."

Now Joseph was in an unprecedented predicament. In those days, two things were true: One, if you were betrothed to someone, you were basically considered already married to them—even before the wedding took place. Joseph and Mary were in this category, and to get out of their betrothal would require a divorce. And two, it was unimaginable to find one's wife was pregnant *before* the marriage was consummated. If by some crazy chance you did find your wife in such a state, you had the right to divorce her (and some scholars even say a spouse would have the right to stone her to death). Thankfully, Joseph wasn't a man to throw stones. The passage says that although Joseph was planning on divorcing Mary, he was a "just" man and "unwilling to put her to shame." He had good intentions. He planned to do what he thought was best without being as cruel as he could have been. By worldly standards, a quiet divorce would have been the generous route to take with her. But God would call on Joseph's patience and confidence—and especially his faith— in a way that had never been seen before. The assurance of an angel led Joseph to change his mind and stay. He persevered through the unprecedented situation and continued to love Mary with an unrelenting love because he had confidence and hope in *God's* direction over his life, even when it didn't make sense. Can you picture what our lives, and this world, would be had Joseph not chosen an unrelenting love?

Hope-Fueled Love Isn't Blind

Perhaps this all sounds pretty risky to you. Why hope for good things to turn out when the past seems to show a bad track record? Isn't that just blind wishful thinking? Well, wishful thinking is certainly blind. But *hope* isn't blind or ignorant. It's different from wishful thinking because it's informed and intelligent. It sees the circumstances and knows the logical way things *should* work out in a fallen world, but it believes for something better. For something more life-giving. Why? Because hope is from God. That may not mean the circumstance turns out exactly the way you want it to, but it does mean God breathed life into *something* during the process. We hope in a God who will *always* do that, whether that's breathing new life into the situation itself or simply into *us* as we walk through it.

For example, let's say there's a spouse at the end of her rope. She chooses to fight for hope, even with full awareness of everything her marriage is facing. She knows the history of mutual disappointment and betrayal. She remembers every season of counseling when hope was anchored in tools and solutions. This wife clearly understands what should logically happen to couples after being disconnected for such a long time. But she hopes. She fully expects God to restore this marriage. Why is she hopeful? Or maybe you're wondering *how* is she hopeful? She is hopeful because she knows God is greater than the reality of her marriage. She has made a choice to anchor her expectation in the God that is the "God of hope" and fills us with joy and peace so we "may abound in hope" (Rom. 15:13), not just in this marriage situation but in all situations in her life. Because her hope is in *God* and not anyone else's behavior or choices, this woman is freed to love people better. When her hope becomes anchored in Christ, she can love others without putting her hope in them. And the same goes for us. Yes, we can hope relationships get better and reconciliation happens, but we hope *in* the Lord. When people inevitably fail, our love can remain steady because our hope remains steady. It may sound like an unrealistic dream, but it's really possible.

I've learned this truth many times over, and I continue to learn. *One of the most freeing feelings is to love someone from the certainty I have in God rather than with the necessity of another person's "good" behavior.* By the way, this doesn't exempt me from disappointment—I feel the sting when a friend wounds me. That's not something to ignore or dismiss, and sometimes lovingly confronting someone who routinely hurts you is necessary for their own spiritual and emotional development. But I place my hope in the God who protects me from the devastation that comes when I set my hope in human relationships. He's the one who best tends to my wounds. So, when I say, "Love doesn't lose hope," it's because my hope is anchored in God. I don't lose hope in God. When I say love is

> One of the most freeing feelings is to love someone from the certainty I have in God rather than with the necessity of another person's "good" behavior.

unrelenting, I am not speaking of personal willpower, nor am I saying it's my responsibility to ensure all of my relationships "last." I am saying love is unrelenting because it endures even when relationships suffer. When I have been hurt, I have the supernatural ability to continue to love in a way that pleases God and reflects His love for me. Said another way, even if the relationship doesn't pan out the way I want, I can still be loving in my posture toward that person, and that posture can be genuine. And if it's possible for me, it's possible for you.

How Does This Show Up in Real Life?

Example 1

Let's say a particularly critical sibling or parent says something that hurts. And worse, they have a track record for being this way. You know they have the shortcuts and passwords to your triggers. Everything in you wants to either rise up and respond with a good honey-dagger comment or shut down and pray until the visit ends while you secretly stew long enough to make a tough roast tender (a little southern homage for y'all). You hear what they say; then the Spirit of God tells you what they *mean*. He says, "They're hurting," "They're insecure," or "This isn't about you." You then have an important internal conversation with the Spirit to debate whether He's right and if there's any room for you to respond the way you *really want to*. Oh wait. Maybe that's just me. Well, you get it. God will both meet you in the moment of pain, assuring you that He sees you, and challenge you to love the way He loves regardless of the other person's behavior.

Example 2

Let's say a trusted friend says something during an argument that is considered "off limits." Something only he or she knows about you is now being weaponized. And it's not the first time this friend has crossed the line into that territory. All your self-protection alarms are ringing at high alert. You have all of the "Why would you?" and "How could you?" and "This is why . . ." comebacks ready. If you're like me, your first response is counterattack. I want to protect myself and I want to win. But if you're not like me, your response may be withdrawal or passive-aggressiveness (where you talk to others or become petty).

But then something happens, and it alters your trajectory. It changes the routine of your typical response. It breaks the cycle—even if you're the only one who notices. It's *divine, unrelenting love.* It's like God speaks softly: "Wait." You can hear Him speaking to you and asking you if you should respond the way you plan to. He poses questions in your spirit like, "Are you hearing what they mean or just what they say?" or "Are you thinking about their story?" He gently reminds you that *He* is the cure for the pain you're feeling—not the right words or actions from your friend. *He's* the one who can breathe the life into you that you need—whether they do or not. And it gives you the moment you need to give them the benefit of the doubt and bear with them a little longer. Where the rest of the world would walk away from that conversation fuming, break out the scorecard of the many times they've done this before, or replay the words to stir up even more anger, a patient and confident love takes over and helps you do something unexpected: Stick around. Keep at it. Love them anyway. With resilient love.

It may require calmly asking follow-up questions to clarify something or praying for them later when the frustration has died down, but in the end, loving someone with hope and resilience means inviting God to guide every response and decision. It's the only way to persevere.

Rules of Thumb

So, how can you love in a resilient, unrelenting way? In a way that bears with a friend, holds out hope, remains patient, and sticks around? In a way that expresses *agape* all over again?

Here are four rules of thumb for any situation:

1. Pursue first.
2. Pursue often.
3. Pursue surrender.
4. Pursue prayer and Scripture.

You've heard that first one before. We explored it a little bit in the last chapter. But it bears repeating because it always pays off. One of the most humbling things God will call us to do is to initiate love toward another person when we would rather withhold it and to consistently offer love rather than give it an expiration date. In His infinite kindness and knowledge, He invites us to imitate Him in this way. He also wants us to invite Him into the process. God will show you what it looks like to make the first move in every scenario.

As for number 2, God will show you how to be consistent in your pursuit, and He will be the reason we can embrace a relentless love. Going first isn't a one-time thing. You have to do it often. You may experience a day when you find yourself handling multiple conflicts—one with your spouse regarding your schedules when you wake up, another with your child who fights you on her outfit for the day, and yet another with your coworker who always makes work more difficult than it needs to be. In all three scenarios, go first. Keep going first. With the next person and the next. Close the gap, just as God did with you. That's unrelenting love at work.

You're probably thinking, *how exhausting*. And you're right. In our own strength, we *will* get exhausted from trying to manage countless relational failures by ourselves. Which leads to numbers 3 and 4.

Number 3 is important. You really can't do numbers 1 and 2 without it. Pursuing surrender means you have to give up control to God on what happens with that person, even as you move back toward them to mend the relationship. Going first is one thing. But going first with an agenda that *this person must respond the way I need them to* is another thing, and it never goes well.

You have to surrender the results of your efforts. You show up and do the right thing—work to move toward them and reestablish the relationship (which sometimes, yes, means telling them how they made you feel as you seek restoration)—and you let them decide what they will do with it. You cannot force a certain outcome. They may respond well; they may not. You cannot control that part, and you have to release it to God, or you won't be able to love in an unrelenting way.

Number 4 is a safe place to run when you'd rather just call it quits in certain relationships. When you need fuel to keep at it, run to God in prayer and *ask* Him for it. He's the originator of this kind of love, and He can give it to you in full measure. More than that, He can channel it through you to others. He knows you need His power, and He delights to give it to you in your time of need. So ask Him for help and search His Word. It will give you the perspective and power you need to keep loving in an unrelenting way.

And isn't that what the world is dying for? A love that lasts? That *hopes all things* even when you feel hopeless. We have that in Christ. God is this way with us every day. So let's offer that to those around us and see just how much this new way of loving might bring people closer to Him.

Prayer: *Lord, thank You for your unrelenting love, and thank You for showing me what it looks like through Your chosen servants like Joseph. I want to love in a way that doesn't give up. I want to be resilient and hopeful in the way I love others, but it's hard and sometimes terrifying. Grant me peace, courage, and faith to love in a way that supersedes my human limitations and is so clearly divine it points people to a perfect God who loves perfectly. Amen.*

Chapter 9

BE REAL: Love Is Honest

'm sitting here with a headache from crying so many tears after watching the movie *Caste*. I have read most of Isabel Wilkerson's book by the same name, but most recently the movie has been brought to life by the director Ava DuVernay. As I'm watching the movie, although I'm familiar with most of what's being told, I find myself overwhelmed by a story told near the end of the film. A young black boy is a part of an otherwise all-white Little League baseball team. The team is made up of energetic nine- and ten-year-olds, and they've just won the championship. The year is 1951.

The movie depicts the team having the privilege to go and swim at a local community pool on a hot summer day after winning a championship, which they are very proud of. When they get there, they realize that the black teammate is not allowed to swim in the pool with them. He is given a blanket and sits in his clothes outside the fence and watches his teammates and all of their parents enjoy a day at the pool. The *Huffington Post,* in a July 2010 article titled "Pools and Politics" regarding the incident writes,

> In Youngstown, Ohio in 1951 the winning Little League team decided that a fitting way to celebrate the victory was a trip to the local swimming pool. When coaches and the players and their families arrived at the pool, one player was not permitted to enter. The child, Al Bright, was asked to sit on the lawn outside the pool area. Several parents took issue with the lifeguards who were enforcing the pool's no-negro policy. The guards finally agreed to a concession. Everyone else got out of the pool. Little Al was put in a rubber raft and a lifeguard pushed him around the pool on the raft. Wiltse writes that Al was specifically told not to touch the water.[6]

Maybe it's because Al was close in age to my kids, or maybe it's because the story is so intimate, but for whatever reason, after watching the scene, my heart broke wide open. The story is being retold by one of his white teammates in the present day, and even hearing him wrestle with what he was witnessing as a young boy breaks my heart. He didn't know what to do with what he was experiencing, nor did he know how to help his friend, young Al. Now more than sixty years later, he still carries the guilt of what he witnessed and now feels like he participated in. But really, what was a nine-year-old boy to do with the complexity of what he was involuntarily a part of?

Naturally, my mind turns toward the question, How in the world can love really overcome such innate sin in the human heart?

It seems that no matter where we are, whether our skin color is the same or not, something in the human heart wants to find ways to differentiate itself from others. Our pride, our greed, and our entitlement partner with the darkness of our sin nature and drive us to find opportunities to exert power over others. We naturally look for ways to elevate and/or differentiate ourselves from others based on the prevailing values of our community. It may be hair color, it may be lineage, it may be zip code, income level, skin color, language, education, region, religion, political affiliation, and so many other distinguishing factors. Remember, in a fallen world with its fallen systems, the highest-ranking class is not the only class to blame. Every class that is not the lowest-ranking class has to do its part to carry the expectations and maintain the health of the system. We all do our part because it's who we are.

If you are black in America, my primary context, this might be hard to see because you might always find yourself in the position with the least amount of power. Maybe you can relate because you've been treated as "lesser" due to your ethnicity. Or maybe for you it's not your ethnicity, but it *is* some other way you feel sidelined, overlooked, or mistreated. You could be the only one in your household who does all the tedious, unseen work that no one else wants to do, and no one thanks you for. You could be the colleague who always carries the weight of the team. You could be one of the few women in a sector of society occupied mostly by men. Or maybe you're in a marriage where you feel you have no voice. However it looks, each of us has some sort of environment where we feel like we have the least amount of power.

But if we think just a little deeper, we can find ourselves in various other environments (social, educational, career, personal, etc.) in which we are *in* a position of power. Maybe we're the most educated in the room or in the family. Maybe we are the married one in a group of singles in a culture that idolizes marriage. Maybe we are the ones with kids among those still praying for that. Maybe we even leave our zip code, traveling to other cities and countries that are less developed, and we realize that as Americans we are considered to hold positions of power even if we don't feel that way in our daily lives. No matter what type of power or influence we have, the reality is *the human condition—which we all inherit and experience—is by default set against the dignifying, equalizing, sacrificial love for all that God calls us to.*

What must we do with that? How do we wrestle with the reality that our nature is in opposition to the kind of love God calls us to express every day? We know our love for others should be curious, free, brave, and resilient. But what do we do when our own internal nature fights against being those very things?

Honest and Humble

We do this: we get honest with God and ourselves, which leads to humility, and we confess. What do I mean by honesty? While honesty or awareness about the way we're wired or the life we have lived up until now is helpful, I'm talking about a different kind of honesty. This is a different, deeper kind of honesty that most of us don't want to deal with. It's the kind of honesty that admits that even on our best day there is a darkness in our heart that naturally leans toward any opportunity to come out ahead. It's the kind of honesty that admits, *The reason I'm so frustrated in the places I feel overlooked isn't always about getting to equal standing with those around me. It's ultimately because I like to be in the position of power. I'm not actually upset that there is a power dynamic going on; I'm just upset that I happen not to be the one at the top of it. Because if I were, I would do better than everyone else has ever done.*

Have you ever gotten *that* honest with God? Or yourself? When you do, you end up becoming something the world can't make sense of: humble. And as opposed to constantly prideful people, humble people are the best to be around. They aren't curated or fake. They're *real*.

If you haven't gotten this honest with God, have you ever considered that this is the reason loving others is so hard? It's hard to love people you want power over. It's hard to love people you think, deep down, are beneath you, even though you happen to be in a position beneath them. It's hard to love people you don't see yourself as equals with—rather, you see yourself as *better than*. It's hard to engage your neighbor according to God's instructions when you are more concerned about power than love.

Have you ever just told God these things—straight out, as honestly as possible, no sugarcoating it? Have you ever just confessed the truth of these things in prayer? Because the ugly truth is that this sort of sin is in *every* human heart. You are no exception, and neither am I. And here's how I know.

The First Power Struggle

In the beginning of time, the world had no power struggles. For some unknown, brief time Adam and Eve had perfect relational communion with God, enjoying His world and His love. Harmony ruled the day. Can you imagine that—relationships with no friction? No conflicts? No hurt feelings or issues to sort through? That was the world before sin entered it.

So, what caused the world to lose this perfect environment of love and relational harmony? As the story goes, the serpent tempted Eve to eat from a tree that God had instructed her and Adam not to eat from. What would eating the fruit do, exactly, according to the serpent? "When you eat it your eyes will be opened and you will be like God, knowing good and evil" (Gen. 3:5).

That was the promise the serpent tempted her with: *you will be like God*. In other words, you can have a power you didn't even know existed. The serpent spoke to some desire in Eve for *more*. That desire was likely dormant until an opportunity presented itself, but it's rooted in some level of dissatisfaction with one's current state. Wanting more only happens when we feel like we don't have enough.

As the rest of the story tells us, Eve ate the fruit and gave some to Adam. He ate it too (Gen. 3:6). They had a world of experiencing perfect love, but it wasn't enough, and they thought they could pursue power without consequence. When they gave into the temptation to try to be God themselves, they learned quickly that a pursuit in power causes unthinkable damage to our relationship with God.

This choice brought sin and strife into the world for the first time. And the ripple effects not only fractured their relationship with God; it fractured their relationship with each other. When God approaches them and asks them about their disobedience, instead of being honest and humbly confessing, they start playing the blame game to get the moral high ground, Adam blaming Eve and Eve blaming the serpent (Gen 3:11–13), and we've been blaming others for our problems ever since.

We are all guilty of the unhealthy pursuit of the power that comes with trying to be God. Instead of experiencing God's love, we grasp for the "better," "higher" seat above others. This is the human condition, and not one of us is exempt from it.

We are all guilty of the unhealthy pursuit of the power that comes with trying to be God.

God's Love Is Possible with God's Help

This moment in the garden of Eden—the one I just walked through—is exactly why humans would rather be in the position of power with the freedom to choose whether we help our neighbor than be in a position that needs the help. Knowing this forces us to face a harsh reality, which is this: *We are not trying to embrace God's standard and example of love from some "middle ground" where we're doing okay but could be doing better. We are attempting to love others from such a place of deficit that only divine power can help us walk in it.*

Here's another way of saying it: You can't love well without God. You cannot be curious, free, and brave, and resilient in the way you love others by your own strength. You'll burn out. You'll end up resentful or jealous because others aren't doing the same for you. You'll get annoyed and you'll start keeping score with others around you because they aren't responding the way you want them to. All of which points to the fact that you want the power over them and control over the outcome of the relationship with them more than you want to love them. See what I mean? It's impossible to live out God's kind of love—the *agape* Jesus modeled for us and our Father requires of us—from a heart that has no natural inclination to do it.

The bottom line is you cannot love according to God's standard without God's help. This should make you feel unqualified and relieved at the same time. Unqualified in your own ability—because you just can't love people well on your own. But relieved, too—because now you don't have to keep trying to muster up the strength to do it by yourself. *You're not expected to do this by yourself.* God expects you to need Him in this work of loving others because God's the only one who can actually love like this. And He has all the empowerment you need, if you'd only come to Him for it.

So, how do you come to Him for it?

Get Honest and Confess

Go back to Psalm 139 (vv. 1–6) and read Psalm 51. Don't forget, God already knows you, so you aren't going to surprise Him with your deep confessions. But the more honest and real you are with Him, the more you prepare your heart to say yes to Him. Don't make the mistake of shallow confession. God already knows anyway. Be specific and tell God where you know you've missed the mark. Confession keeps our humanity before us. It helps us remember we are the fallen creatures who need the help, and God is the Creator who desires to give it to us. Confession also reminds us that we don't do all of this for applause or to impress anyone; we do it because we love God, who first loved us.

Remind Yourself of the Gospel

In the moments it feels especially hard to love others—the moments we'd rather have the power seat instead of doing the harder work of love—one of the most effective ways to choose God's way instead of our own way is remembering the gospel. Remembering our own story of how God saved us and the work He's done in our lives all along the journey should bring tears to our eyes and grace to our hearts for others. It should return us to a place of humility, gratitude, and joy. God did not opt for a power play when He saw us flailing. We offended God worse than anyone could offend us, and what did He do? He reached out to us in love through Christ. He sent His beloved Son to us. *Even while we were running away and living as enemies of God.* When we were at our worst, doing the unthinkable and unforgivable, He offered Himself on the cross to cover us. He came not as a high and mighty strategist in a power seat; He came in the most *un*powerful seat the world has ever seen. And if Jesus lived and loved in a humble way, why do you and I think we're exempt from this rule?

That's the gospel, and it's unbelievable. It's incredible. It is a divine love the world had never known before Christ and could not understand at first glance. This gospel, the love it models, and in turn requires, is the only thing that can bring hope to the heart of humans caught in their own condition. When you find yourself caught in that condition, my friend, remember the gospel. It will remind you how God loved you before He ever asked you to love someone else. There's no love like gospel love; it is the ultimate demonstration of *agape.*

Remind Yourself of the Power You Already Have

Remind yourself that you have Jesus as your Savior and the Holy Spirit as your power source. Those things were given to you the moment you became a Christian. Which means that although the call to love well is certainly weighty, it does not weigh you down. Why? Because your newness in Christ also delivers a new nature. It doesn't totally replace that sinful, prideful proclivity, but it certainly creates a worthy opponent and promises a guaranteed victory in the end.

Said another way, *I now have the nature of Christ in me to combat the nature of sin. That is the only hope in changing the effect of the human condition.* Before I see change, this newness births unexplainable gratitude that God has given Himself to help me live in such a way that is contrary to my nature. It gives me hope because I have a Father who does not expect me to do this without His help. And then I have courage to do what seems scary—what may disrupt everything that's comfortable for me. I have to ask God for an openness to see opportunities to love that would not even register with me if I'm limiting myself to minor improvements rather than significant overhaul.

On the days it feels impossible to love according to God's standards, remind yourself: *Christ is already in me. He dwells within me through the power of His Spirit, which means He can love through me.* It is possible for divine love to flow through me to others because divine love already lives inside of me.

Ask for New Perspective

Another helpful prayer to pray when you don't feel like loving someone (or it's just exhausting and overwhelming) is this: *God, give me new eyes for new perspective.* New eyes to see ourselves, to see where we have yet to learn about ourselves so we can see clearly how we perceive

> **It is possible for divine love to flow through me to others because divine love already lives inside of me.**

others in the world around us. New perspective to see what you're refining in me. New eyes to see the situation of the other person the way *God* sees it. With compassion and understanding and a renewed mind and a heart of tenderness that focuses on the good instead of the bad. Isn't that what you want in a moment when you have really messed up and feel particularly unlovable? As His child, ask God to help you see through those kind of eyes—even when looking at your worst enemy in their worst moment; that's when you start looking more like Christ.

Get around Some People on the Same Path

We know we are made for community. We thrive in healthy groups and partnership with people who share our priorities about living for God. Find (or pray for) some people to walk this journey with you (not *for* you) so you can sharpen and encourage one another. Connect with peers who relate to you and some seasoned, faithful people who can *lead* you. If you don't have that, ask God to bring safe and wise people to you. Then use those "new eyes" to see when they show up. If you're determined to love at the highest level, it's great to have a community of people with the same determination.

Honest and Humble with Others

You'll find that as you pursue these topics, your relationships will start changing because *you're* changing. It's just the way divine love works: as you get honest and humble with God on a regular basis, you start becoming honest and humble with others. And that's a whole new way to love when you think about it. After all, when relationships hit a difficult point, our world doesn't get honest and humble; it gets *dis*honest and power hungry.

When an offense or hurtful situation happens, most people immediately run to some form of dishonesty, deflection, or blame. Instead of just honestly telling the truth as it stands in a certain situation—owning their part to play in the hurtful situation and then communicating the ways they feel hurt by the other person—half-truths start spilling out. People typically minimize their part to play and maximize the other person's faults, they exaggerate what happened to favor how they are perceived, or they simply lie about the facts of the situation to avoid admitting their own mistakes. Why? Because they feel helpless, and they are grasping for an external appearance of the moral high ground—for the position of power. (And when I say "they," I mean "we," because the truth is, we've all done this at some point.)

Loving in the divine way is different. It doesn't have to minimize, maximize, exaggerate, or lie in any given relational dispute. It doesn't have to put on a fake front. It can just be honest and accurate—in a relational dispute, yes, but in any conversation really. When you've made a habit of being honest and humble with God, you start handling *all* your relationships that way. It's a whole new way to love others compared to the typical approaches seen in our culture, and it's something that can make people wonder how you are able to be so different. So *real* in a world where everyone else is putting on a mask. While everyone else is reaching for power, God's love empowers you not to want it anymore.

Let's Wrap It Up

As we close out this final chapter, I can't emphasize enough how important honesty and humility are in the pursuit of *agape* (love). We have identity and a stability in God that is so strong we shouldn't feel the need to exert our power in a way that's not pleasing to Him. As Christians we are declared royal, invaluable, and purposeful by the one true God. There's nothing on this earth—no status, no title, no position, no wealth—that is more important than who God says we are. Because of that, we don't have to spend our energy belittling others or finding ways to elevate ourselves. We cannot walk in insecurity masked by false pride and simultaneously pursue divine love. If you want to do this "love" thing well, you're going to have to invite God to search your heart for even the slightest slivers of arrogance so that you can *agape* well. When you do, you'll find yourself enjoying God at a deeper level and loving others in a whole new way.

Prayer: *Father, You see even the smallest trace of pride in my heart. You know when my fear of negative perception or actual rejection begins to affect the way I love. Please remind me of the satisfaction I have in You so that I won't look for meaningless power in other places. Lord, stir up humility and honesty in me so that I can love with total dependence on You. Bring people to my path who want to love the same way. Thank You for the countless chances You give me as I commit to trying this new way to love. In Jesus's name, amen.*

Conclusion

A New Way to Love

Well, you did it. You got to the end. How do you feel? Depending on how quickly you took all this information in, and how new it was to you, it may feel overwhelming. Before you head back out into the world equipped with tons of new information, let's look at what we've covered and think about next steps.

First, as you process part 1, spend some time asking God to show you what your limits on love are, and ask Him to remove them one by one.

- **Chapter 1:** Have you completely grasped the idea of *agape*? It's different from our world's approach to love. Do you have some incorrect definitions of love that need to be unpacked?
- **Chapter 2:** When it comes to your definitions of love prior to reading this book,

in what ways have you settled for lesser
forms of love instead of God's best definition of sacrificial, *agape* (love)?

- **Chapter 3:** Maybe you've had some tendencies throughout your life to choose
partial instead of whole when it comes
to the way you love God and others.
Partial love is the way we try to protect
ourselves from getting hurt rather than
trusting God. When it comes to categories of heart, soul, mind, and strength,
which part do you typically hold back
from God?

- **Chapter 4:** Do you ever try to *give agape*
before *receiving* it from your heavenly
Father? If so, it may be because there's a
significant way that your earthly father
experience impacts you, holding you
back from fully receiving God's love. Do
you understand what gaps your earthly
father created for you? Are you aware
of how they affect the way you receive
love *from* God, give love *to* God, and love
others?

Understanding how these limits have shown up in your
life will lead to greater self-awareness, greater understanding
of God's love, and deeper gratitude for how He has offered it
freely and completely.

Second, while you're processing the way you limit love (because everything in this book is an ongoing continuous process), you can begin to think about how you love others. There's a lot to consider.

- **Chapter 5:** Do you need to be more curious about God, others, and yourself? Have you missed out on the power of knowing someone's story? You can find new ways to learn more about the people God has asked you to love every time you're with them and even when you're not. Remember, in a world where people are typically disinterested in others (and God) unless it pays off in some way, being curious is a new and divine way to love.

- **Chapter 6:** Then there is the forgiveness issue. It is such a burden for so many of us, and maybe you've tried to forgive or release or heal from something; and it's just not working. You feel stuck. You might consider finding a therapist or a pastor or a trusted mentor who you can talk to about this. You cannot put unforgiveness on a back burner and focus all of your attention on pursuing divine love. Just because a burner is in the back of the stove doesn't mean it uses less energy. If that unforgiveness isn't addressed, it will be a constant drain on your spiritual journey, and God wants you to be free. It's time to release the debt. What person or hurtful experience do you need to release to God?

• **Chapter 7:** The idea that love is brave was revolutionary for me. To realize that it has nothing to do with my personality, strengths, or motivations but has everything to do with taking the initiative and making the first move because God made the first move toward me. It's the risk a person takes every time they invite a stranger or friend to know Jesus. It's the risk a person takes every time they move *toward* a frustrating spouse instead of *away*. Even when it's uncomfortable. We risk rejection every time we share the gospel or confront a friend, but the benefit of a transformed soul or relationship makes it worthwhile. This is the essence of brave love. We know that *agape* will call us to take risks, but we believe the potential of that love being received is worth the risk. *Agape* (love) is okay with the fact that this is uncomfortable, and it has the bravery to push through that discomfort of going first. In what relationship do you need to be brave, even through the discomfort,

and "go first" in the work of reestablish-
ing the connection?

- **Chapter 8:** Resilient love can be scary
because it requires us not only to choose
agape but to choose it over and over again.
Love endures and never fails. *Agape* is so
powerful it covers our mistakes. If we
mess up (or someone else messes up),
we can try again, and relationships can
be restored. Resilient love doesn't fade
easily and isn't scared off by hard things.
In what ways have you shied away from
being unrelenting in your love for God
and others? In what daily relationships
have you given up after one or two tries?
Take some time to ask God to remind you
of the ways He has shown you unrelenting love, and ask Him to help you express
this same love to those around you. In a
world where most people give up when it
gets hard to keep loving, resilient love is
not only new and different; it's refreshing.
- **Chapter 9:** Finally, *agape* is a type of love
that has to be honest, transparent, and
covered in humility. We live in a world
that grasps for the power seat—to always
try to be higher than others—but *agape*
has the ability to go low, to be humble.
It's a whole new kind of love. In which

relationship have you found yourself often trying to "go higher" than the other person? With what person do you typically try to take the moral high ground? With what person do you tend not to be honest when you're in a dispute (i.e., minimizing, maximizing, exaggerating, etc.)? More importantly, in what ways do you find yourself not being totally honest with God when you run up against your own inabilities or failures? What would being totally honest with God look like for you?

I know all of this can seem like one long unachievable checklist. But it's really not. It is a full descriptive picture of what God's love is already doing in us and has already been doing since the beginning of time. Now He is equipping us to do the same, even in our imperfections, so that people might see Him in us.

After all that I'll leave you with a last word: find a good community to surround yourself with (and *be* community for someone else). *Don't do this alone.* The ultimate goal is not for someone to thank us for loving well or for us to congratulate ourselves for forgiving someone. The ultimate goal is that we love God more and point people to Him by the way we love them, and we do it through humility, forgiveness, seeking to understand, grace, patience, kindness, a willingness to try again, and a determination never to quit.

In a world stuck in all its old ways of relating to those around them, this is the new way to love your neighbor. It's God's way, and it never fails.

The Gospel Is the Real First Step to the New Way to Love

I believe everything in this book is good and helpful information and I am trusting the Lord to put it in the right hands and hearts. But all of what is shared in this book is based on a foundation of surrender to Jesus as Lord. Without that surrender, you can not have true, or lasting, transformation. This kind of surrender includes the acknowledgment of the gap between you and God (confession) and an invitation for Jesus to bridge that gap (surrender). If you haven't ever done that, here's a simple prayer to get you started. Make it your own.

Even if it feels awkward, be authentic before God.

> *God, I know that You desire a relationship with me. I know You desire true worship and committed love from me. I also know that on my own, I can never offer those things to You. I know that only Jesus can fill the gap between You and me. I confess that I have, and always will, fall short of Your standard when I try to do it on my own. I'm sorry for every time I have ignored You and chosen my own way. Right now, I choose Jesus as Savior. I surrender my entire being, heart, soul, mind, and strength to*

Jesus as Lord over my life. I surrender to You as the perfect Father who offered His perfect Son for all of my imperfections. Thank You for the gift of the Holy Spirit that comes with this surrender. Show me the new way—Your way— in every area of my life. I never want to try to do it without You again. Thank You for Your patience and grace. Keep me amazed by it. In Jesus's name, amen.

Now you can truly be on a path to loving your neighbor, but more important, you'll experience an outpouring of God's love for you. Without complete submission to *His way of life* you can never fully embrace this new *way to* love.

Notes

1. J. I. Packer, *Knowing God* (Carol Stream, IL: IVP, 2023).

2. "psuché," Bible Hub, https://biblehub.com/greek/5590.htm (accessed August 29, 2024).

3. "ichus," Bible Hub, https://biblehub.com/greek/2479.htm (accessed August 29, 2024).

4. Sandra L. Richter, *The Epic of Eden: A Christian Entry into the Old Testament* (Old Saybrook, CT: Tantor Audio, 2018).

5. Richter, *The Epic of Eden*.

6. Kate Kelly, "Pools and Politics," *Huffington Post*, July 16, 2010, updated May 25, 2011, https://www.huffpost.com/entry/pools-and-politics_b_648781.